LIFE AFTER DEATH

D0888971

LIFE AFTER DEATH

Abbeydale Press

ISBN: 978-1-86147-256-4

1 3 5 7 9 10 8 6 4 2

Published by Abbeydale Press
An imprint of Bookmart Limited
Registered Number 2372865
Trading as Bookmart Limited
Blaby Road, Wigston
Leicestershire, LE18 4SE

Originally incorporated in *The Encyclopedia of the
Unexplained* and *Mysteries of the Mind* published by
Bookmart Limited.

Production by Omnipress Ltd, Eastbourne

Printed in Great Britian

CONTENTS

GHOSTS AND
APPARITIONS

A troubled lady, haunting the place she was bound to in life; a dead father, unable to rest easy until his will is carried out; a piratical sailor whose love of adventure defeats even death – the many shades of ghosts present intriguing, if inconsistent, evidence for survival beyond the grave.

In 1968, Frances Little and her husband were delighted with the adobe house they had bought in the desert setting of California's Kern County, but after a few weeks, Mr Little became disturbed at seeming to see his wife in two places at once. He'd leave her in one room, or outside, only to see her immediately afterwards, wandering around at the other end of the house. Finally, it dawned on him that the 'other woman' must be a ghost. But whose ghost? And why was she haunting the house?

Then, alone at home one night, Frances Little herself saw a 'tall thin woman in a long dark old-fashioned dress' come out of a back room and go into her bedroom. From there, she went into the family room and Mrs Little was able to see her features quite clearly.

Not long after this, Mrs Little was sorting through some junk that had been left in the garage by the previous owners. To her amazement, she came across a photograph of a woman who looked exactly like the ghost she had seen. Careful enquiries revealed that this was Alice Margaret Kolitisch who, with her husband, had had the adobe house built in the 1920s. She was, Frances Little felt, still concerned about the house she had loved when alive.

This is a ghost story in a classic mould: the troubled shade of the dead haunts a place it had been bound to emotionally in life. But not all ghost stories are like this, and because hauntings are so varied in kind, they make intriguing, if inconsistent, evidence for some kind of life after death.

Legend says that US President Abraham Lincoln had a strong belief in ghosts: he apparently consulted a medium during the worst days of the American Civil War and, according to W.H. Crook, one of his bodyguards, Lincoln had a number of psychic experiences. At the beginning of April 1865, he told Crook that he had had a dream in which he had been in the hall of the White House, and had seen a coffin draped in black there. When he asked who it was for, he was told: 'The president.'

On 11 April, Lincoln told Crook that he had dreamed of his own assassination; and on the morning of 14 April he had a vision of a ship carrying him to some unknown place. That night, against the advice of Crook and other members of his staff, Lincoln went to Ford's Theater in Washington. There, he was shot dead by John Wilkes Booth. Within months of Lincoln's death, rumours began to circulate that his ghost was haunting the White House.

Lincoln's spectre took a long time to take visible form. Theodore Roosevelt, president from 1901 to 1909, maintained that he 'felt the presence' of Lincoln at 1600 Pennsylvania Avenue. The first person actually to see his ghost was Grace Coolidge, wife of Calvin Coolidge, the 30th president, who was in office between 1923 and 1929. Mrs Coolidge saw the ghost standing at the window of the Oval Office, staring out on to Pennsylvania Avenue in the attitude of a man deep in thought. Staff members and presidential aides have reported the same thing – and the apparition always appears at the same window.

The next president, Herbert Hoover (at the White House from 1929 to 1933), heard no more than 'odd sounds' but said that 'many of them were fantastic'.

Between 1933, when Franklin Delano Roosevelt became president, and 1945, when he died, Lincoln's ghost was allegedly seen many times. On one occasion Queen Wilhelmina of The Netherlands, who had long had an interest in spiritualism, had gone to bed in the Lincoln Room – formerly used by Lincoln himself as a dressing room – when she heard a gentle tap on the door. She opened it, and there stood the dead president, gravely doffing his famous stovepipe hat; then the apparition vanished. When the queen told Roosevelt of her encounter the next morning, he confessed that he knew the

Robert (left) and John F. Kennedy. Both brothers saw the Lincoln spectre at the White House during John's presidency, although neither was noted for his interest in psychic or spiritual matters.

room was haunted; Winston Churchill had also seen the ghost of Lincoln while sleeping there, and Mrs Roosevelt had detected Lincoln's presence on several occasions.

Harry S. Truman, who succeeded to the presidency on Roosevelt's death and lived in the White House from 1945 to 1952, often joked to his guests about Lincoln's ghost. He once admitted that though he had never seen it, he was certain that he had heard it, in the form of footsteps which approached his bedroom door, followed by a knocking.

There had certainly been no rational explanation for these sounds, he said, and they always occurred in the early hours of the morning. A White House stenographer who served both

Roosevelt and Truman allegedly saw Lincoln frequently. The first time was in the Lincoln Room; the spectre was sitting on the bed pulling on his boots. The girl was badly scared, although with repeated appearances she seems to have got used to seeing the ghost. Both John and Robert Kennedy saw the spirit of Lincoln, according to friends of the Kennedy family.

The White House ghost is intriguing for several reasons. First, it hardly seems likely that several presidents, their wives, a queen, and a statesman like Winston Churchill would lie about seeing the wraith of Lincoln: 'seeing ghosts' might call their fitness for high office into question. The credentials of the witnesses, then, are beyond question.

But is this ghost really the spirit of Abraham Lincoln, bound to the scene where he worked and thought so hard and so deeply? Or is the apparition brought into being by something else? Could it be the result of a collective feeling that the White House really ought to be haunted by Lincoln, the greatest of all the men who lived there, and who died so tragically – so that those who have seen him, presidents included, somehow projected the 'spirit' to suit their own unconscious wishes? Or might the apparition be some kind of recording of Lincoln, impressed upon the place somehow and played over and over again? Or is the Lincoln ghost not one ghost, but several – sometimes one thing, sometimes another, depending on the circumstances and the person who perceives it?

Such questions take us to the heart of the mystery surrounding ghosts of all kinds.

HOARSE WHISPERS

What is a ghost? That the belief that a ghost is present and active can be created by circumstances is beyond doubt. Given some specious evidence, a credulous collection of witnesses, and a background of fear, a ghost will make itself heard, seen or felt. This is very clear from the story told by New Zealander Frank Brookesmith, who until his death in 1991 was one of the last few survivors from the age of square-rigged sailing ships.

In his book *I Remember the Tall Ships*, Brookesmith recalled a haunting that briefly afflicted the tanker *Orowaiti* on a voyage across the Pacific from Wellington, New Zealand, to San Francisco, in the early 1920s. What happened was this. After one of the sailors on board the ship had committed suicide, the rest of the crew, understandably distressed at the incident, swore that the dead man was haunting the bow end of the ship. The ghost was invisible, but its constant, eerie whisper could clearly be heard. Determined to find out what was really going on, Brookesmith went forward at about four o'clock one morning to investigate.

'The ship was rolling quite moderately and I paced the deck from right forward to the after rail on the weather side. I heard nothing. I walked along the lee side and paused by the windlass.

'I froze, and the hairs on the back of my neck stood on end… It felt as if all my hair was standing on end. Someone was talking in a hoarse whisper!… I ran down the ladder to the foredeck and I walked into the space under the focsle head. It was all as dark as the inside of a cow but I knew what was there… I stood quite still and listened. There was no sound save the usual creaks and cracks of a ship in a seaway.. .

'I went back… to the after rail and I could hear a faint whispering. I could not distinguish the words but there was no mistaking the sound… My skin crept. I knew that I could easily imagine words but I simply had to find the source of the sounds. I moved about and found that, the nearer I was to the gypsy [a small winch], the clearer was the sound. It was an indistinct asthmatic whisper.

'I put my hand on the [anchor] chain where it went down the pipe into [its] locker and I felt it! As the ship rolled the rusty links moved against each other to make this harsh sound.

'Rub two pieces of rough iron together and you will hear what we heard,' Brookesmith wrote many years later. 'Add to it unhappiness and superstitious fears and you will have a haunting.' He silenced the 'ghost' by lashing the chain down with rope. 'I've found the ghost and I've bound him hands and feet,' he reported with a certain grim satisfaction.

Frank Brookesmith was, on that occasion at least, driven to get to the root of the shipboard 'haunting' partly by curiosity and partly by a determination not to be prey – or to be in thrall – to what he called 'superstitious fears'. But he also told his family of another and quite different experience of the supernatural that he had as a young man, before he went to sea, in the last years of World War One.

He was then working as a clerk in a bank in Christchurch, New Zealand; one of the few perks of the job was a free flat above the bank premises. The perk in turn had its price – which was that he had to be on the alert for any attempt to raid the bank. To help terminally dissuade any villains intent on relieving the bank of its customers' cash – or perhaps simply as a psychological support – he was issued with a hefty British Army officer's .455 Webley revolver and several boxes of ammunition. He used most of the ammunition practising with the pistol in the deserted hills outside the town, but he slept with the weapon loaded at his bedside every night.

One night he awoke suddenly, inexplicably disturbed. Peering warily at first down the length of his bed through half-closed eyes – half-expecting, half-fearing to find an intruder in his room - he found himself staring round-eyed at the figure of a young woman, dressed in white, kneeling as if in prayer beside his bed – and leaning her weightless arms on the covers over his knees.

This apparition, he swore, bore no relation to any image from any dream he had been having immediately prior to waking up. In fact he had been in a dreamless period of sleep when he was so strangely disturbed. What he saw, he admitted, frightened him. But his reaction to this extraordinary sight was weirdly rational: he wondered if it were not some outlandish decoy – the gangster's moll pretending to be a ghost! – set up by some particularly cunning set of burglars. With unusual presence of mind, he reached for his gun. As he swung it into aim, the image of the girl kneeling by his bedside faded away.

Brookesmith found himself rather foolishly waving a heavy revolver at his own bare feet. Making the best of a bad job, he salved his wounded pride by creeping around his flat and then the ground floor – the working area of the bank – looking for any sign of a break-in. He found nothing out of order, but neither could he explain the apparition that had woken him up.

Here we have a witness to two very different kinds of haunting, and a witness, to boot, with a certain rather startlingly logical reaction to both. Unfortunately, we don't know (because he did not say) whether Brookesmith made any attempt to discover if anyone else had ever seen the female phantom that rested so lightly on his bed, or if he made any effort later to find out whose phantom she may have been.

However, the real importance of these two stories, side by side and from the same source, is that someone can on one occasion believe he is really seeing a ghost and accept it as such, and on another occasion, confronted by another apparent haunting, take a thoroughly sceptical view and investigate and effectively exorcise it. To that person – and this is the point – the existence of false ghosts does not preclude the existence of real ones. And no one can say that Brookesmith's extra-ordinarily cool reaction was essentially different from one case to the other. On each occasion he responded according to a

13

certain logic (despite his fright). The witness, if not the phenomenon, was consistent throughout.

DEATH-OMEN

Does any of this get us any nearer the answer to the question: what is a ghost?

In a way, no, this last story does not, because there is no evidence to suggest that the phantom lady seen by the conscientious bank guard and bluff, no-nonsense sailor Frank Brookesmith was not, in any case, a figment of his own momentarily disorientated imagination. But it does tell us that the most sceptical and practical of people can believe that they have genuinely seen a ghost. In short, the key to ghost stories may be the witness, not the ghost. And these two stories

The spectral coach and coachman, of whom it has been said that 'scarcely an old road in England' lacks an example. But how does a coach acquire a 'spiritual' form, if ghosts are the shades of the dead?

together also tell us that the most common presumption about ghosts is that they are the spirits – or at least the inexplicably immaterial records – of people once alive and now dead.

Before sorting out the vexed question of the role of the witness in ghost reports, it's as well to establish how varied the phenomenon of hauntings itself can be.

Ghosts of people may or may not be images of the spirit world, but they are not always apparitions of dead people, or even of animals.

Christina Hole comments in *Haunted England*: 'There is scarcely an old road in England along which the Spectral Coach has not trundled at some time or another. It may be either a genuine coach or a hearse; but whatever form it takes, it bears certain distinguishing marks [that] prove it to be something from another world. It is always black, and so are the driver and his horses. Often both are headless. It appears suddenly on the roadway and moves very fast and usually without noise. Only in a few cases do we hear of the rumble of wheels on the road or the clattering of horses' hoofs to give warning of its approach. Like most apparitions of its kind, it… often serves as a death-omen for those unlucky enough to encounter it.'

Why vehicles should take on spectral form, no one knows (let alone how), but phantom conveyances appear time and again in accounts of ghosts and hauntings. Furthermore, this is a tradition that refuses to die (so to speak). Modern accounts of ghost vehicles are rife with phantom trains, buses, ships, cars, and even aircraft.

SPECTRAL SHIP

In the winter of 1942, the destroyer USS *Kennison* was returning from an antisubmarine patrol along the California coast, coming up to the Golden Gate at the mouth of San

Francisco Bay, when a heavy fog came out of nowhere. The *Kennison's* engine-room bells rang for dead slow, and the ship began to nose carefully through the water, its foghorn sounding.

Then the fantail lookout, torpedoman Jack Cornelius, yelled into the ship's tannoy for everyone to look aft. Cornelius and another seaman, who was on the aft gundeck, both reported that a huge, derelict, two-masted sailing ship had passed within a few feet of the destroyer's stern. They had had the hulk in full view for about half a minute before the fog closed in around it. The radar operators, however, had not seen a thing before, during, or after the sighting of the seemingly immaterial ship.

There is one ghost ship that has been seen dozens of times over the years by sailors. In a letter to *Occult Review* in 1921, F.G. Montagu Powell recounted an incident that had occurred many years previously, when he was serving with the Royal Navy:

'Somewhere in July 1859, when I was on HMS *Euryalus*, we were off the Cape of Good Hope when a curious thing happened. It was about six bells (11 a.m.) in the forenoon, and I was midshipman of the watch, when a dull and heavy mist fell upon us. We were under steam and sail and very light airs from the south were hardly filling our sails, the sun breaking out through the mist like a fiery copper ball every now and then, when we sighted a sailing ship right ahead of us, lying in fact right across our track and so close that before we could hail her or alter our course we were on top of her and in fact cut clean through her.

'Her sails seemed to me flat, lifeless and discoloured, no "bellying to the breeze" about them. Her crew, clad in sou'westers and tarpaulins and the traditional breeches, moved lifelessly about the decks, coiling up ropes or leaning over the hammock netting, and paying not the slightest attention to us, not nearly so much as we paid to them.

Two phantom faces, photographed from on board the oil tanker SS Watertown *in December 1924. The ghost faces apparently had the features of two sailors who had died in an accident on the voyage down the Pacific coast of the USA and had been buried at sea. The faces appeared for days afterwards, though only for brief periods each day.*

'I remember the curious vague look she had as, apparently undamaged by this tremendous impact (though of course there was no impact, it was just like cutting through a shadow or a cloud) she vanished slowly astern, the mist overwhelming and enfolding her like a shroud. I remember hearing one bluejacket saying to another, "Yon's the Flying Dutchman, I expect."'

The Flying Dutchman, Hendrik Vanderdecken, blasphemed against God and was condemned to sail the seas until the Last Judgement. That is a legend. But here we have dates, names, a specific location – and an account of a genuine personal experience. Was this spectral ship the *Flying Dutchman*? Or did the legend spring up to explain all such ghostly encounters at sea?

RECORDINGS OF THE PAST

In their way, steam trains are no less romantic than full-rigged ships – although no less problematic when it comes to explaining how ghost trains could be in any sense 'spiritual'. But there is no lack of them in the annals of ghost lore.

John Quirk, of Pittsfield, Massachusetts, reported that he and several customers at the Bridge Lunch café saw a phantom train hauled by a steam engine one afternoon in February 1958. The train consisted of a baggage car and five or six coaches, which the witnesses described in great detail. A month later, a similar train passed the same location at top speed, barrelling towards Boston, at 6.30 one morning.

Railroad officials insisted that no steam engine had run on that line for years. On yet another occasion when the phantom train was reported, the railroad stated categorically that no train of any material kind had been on that section of track at that time.

As trucks have largely replaced trains for hauling freight – and as the trucker and his big rig have become romanticized as modern exemplars of the great American tradition of rugged individualism – so ghost trucks have appeared on the highways.

In *Fate* magazine for February 1986, truck driver Harriette Spanabel of Brooksville, Florida, recalled an experience that unnervingly echoes Steven Spielberg's eerie movie *Duel*:

'I drive a tractor trailer and haul produce from Florida up the East Coast and west as far as Texas. For the past year and a half, always on my return run, a phantom truck follows me at least part of the time. At first I thought it was my imagination. One minute nothing would be behind me but the next minute a tractor trailer would be there.

'This truck has followed me on both Interstate highways and narrow two-lane roads. It is always behind me at night, moving over every once in a while so that its left headlight hits my left mirror directly. It disappears just as quickly as it appears.

'I now know for sure that I am not imagining the truck because I have a witness who also watched my mystery vehicle. I recently took my friend Kelly Rose with me to Miami to make a delivery. I picked up the load in Philadelphia on March 8, 1985. It was a load of dry freight with two drops. It was when we were coming back from Miami that the truck first joined us at approximately 11:30 the evening of the 12th. I drove out of Lakeland, Fla, on US 98 going north. I planned to turn onto [State Route] 471 which runs through the middle of the Green Swamp. The phantom truck first appeared behind us on US 98 about two miles before I made my turn onto [State Route] 471. It followed us from there until we had almost

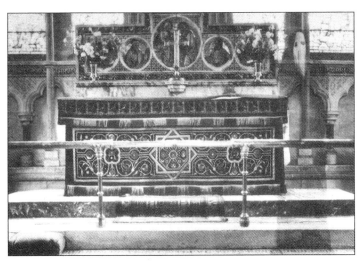

The image of a ghost that appeared in a picture taken inside Newby Church, Yorkshire, by the vicar, the Revd K. F. Lord, in the early 1960s. The ghost was not visible to the priest when he took the photograph.

reached [State Route] 50 where I turn to go west into the town where I live.

'On a narrow two-lane road which runs through a state forest, about 50 miles from my house, the truck again appeared behind us. Kelly immediately asked where it had come from. Of course I couldn't tell her but it followed us for 30 miles before it disappeared this time.

'Kelly, who had been watching the truck intently in her mirror, was astounded. I stopped my truck on 471 and we got out and looked for the other truck. It was completely gone. On this road there are no side roads where a truck could pull on or off. There are no shoulders where a truck could pull off without either tipping over or ending up tangled in a mass of big trees. And let me add there was no other traffic on 471 going in either direction.'

There is no difficulty in believing that these various witnesses are telling the truth – especially as in each case there was more than one witness to the strange events they describe. But these phantoms of the inanimate can hardly be spirits of something dead – since they weren't alive in the first place. So we may be forced to conclude that many ghosts are some kind of recording of the past. But then the problem still remains as to why a particular train, ship or even mighty, snarling 18-wheel semi-trailer should record itself on a particular place: why them, and not any of the hundreds of others that have passed that way?

GHOULISH APPEARANCE

Probably the most frequently told of all kinds of ghost story are those concerning apparitions of people at the moment of their death. Here at least the ghost is inextricably linked with the notion of a life after death – or, at least, with some kind of spiritual existence that is able to project itself across time and space from the dying person to someone near or dear to them. Two instances of this kind of haunting – if that is the word – show how different they can be.

One morning in the spring of 1973, 58-year-old Mrs Martha Beckwhite was doing one of the things she liked best – working in her garden in Blandford, Dorset. Without warning she felt, without knowing how she could identify it, the presence of one of her youngest daughter's friends, Luke Fore. Then, she distinctly heard his voice say 'Goodbye, Martha'. Again without knowing why, she knew that he had died. When the telephone rang in the evening of that day and she heard her daughter's voice on the line, she said: 'Don't worry, darling; I know why you've called. Luke's just died, hasn't he?'

Indeed he had, of cancer of the liver. Two things about this case are intriguing, however. First was that she had met Luke Fore only once or twice (he was the husband of one of her daughter's closest friends at the time). Second was that she had no idea that Luke was ill. For various reasons Luke's cancer had been kept a secret from everyone but his immediate family: no one outside that small circle knew that he even had a cold, let alone was terminally ill.

There are two ways of stating the mystery here. Whatever the ultimate answer, there may be some clue in the fact that Martha Beckwhite and Luke Fore got along famously together on the few occasions that they met, although they were perhaps 20 years apart in age. Why did he appear to her, though, whom he had met but a few times? Or perhaps the problem should be put another way: why and how did she alone of all the people who knew Luke (and many knew him more intimately) 'tune in' to the fact of his death? Whatever the answer, there is no doubt that Martha Beckwhite received and understood, by some paranormal means, a message from someone who was dying, and whom she had no reason to suppose was even remotely at risk of death.

A much more typical case of a near - death apparition was recounted in the October 1957 edition of *Fate* magazine.

Mary Travers was sitting up late waiting for her husband George, who was an insurance salesman, to come home. Shortly after the clock struck 11, she heard a cab coming down the street. It stopped in front of the house, and Mrs Travers heard a voice, presumably the driver's, call out 'Good night!' Then she recognized the familiar sound of her husband's steps on the porch. She hurried to the front door to welcome him home.

He came in silently, with his hat pulled down over his eyes, and then he stood with his back to his wife while she shut the door. She thought he was behaving oddly, and asked did he feel all right? He turned to face her – and in place of George's face she saw a hideous white death-mask. She screamed, and continued to scream, so that the neighbours rushed in to see what was wrong. By then, the apparition had vanished. Minutes later the phone rang: the caller regretfully announced that George Travers had been killed in a train crash.

It is difficult to account for such an apparition except as a spirit of the dead. It seems unlikely that by sheer coincidence Mrs Travers imagined his ghoulish appearance on the very night he died. It makes more sense to assume that the spectre was indeed her husband's spirit, or at least a projection from his mind, sent to warn Mrs Travers – albeit silently and shockingly – of what had happened to him.

THE DEAD MAN'S WILL

The classic example of a haunting that seems to prove the continued existence of an individual in some form after death is the famous case of the 'lost' will of the North Carolina farmer James L. Chaffin. This is one of the best-documented cases in all psychic research. As several writers have remarked, even the lawyers involved seem to have been honest.

James L. Chaffin, a farmer of Davie County, North Carolina, had four sons: John, James, Marshall and Abner. On 16 November 1905 he made a will, attested by two witnesses, leaving everything he owned to his third son, Marshall. Why he singled out Marshall, no one knows. But, a little over 13 years later, the old man had a change of heart. He made a new will. It read:

'After reading the 27th chapter of Genesis I, James L. Chaffin, do make my last will and testament and here it is. I want, after giving my body a decent burial, my little property to be equally divided between my four children... and if she is living, you must take care of your mummy. Witness my seal and hand. James L. Chaffin. This January 16, 1919.'

This second will lacked the signatures of any witnesses, but would be legally valid under the laws of North Carolina if it could be established that the whole of the document was in the testator's own handwriting. Chaffin, unknown to anyone at the time, put the will between two pages of the family Bible on which were printed the 27th chapter of Genesis. The paper was folded over to make a kind of pocket. Chaffin never mentioned the second will to anyone, but he did scribble on a roll of paper, which he stitched into an inside pocket of his overcoat, a note that said: 'Read the 27th chapter of Genesis in my daddie's old Bible.'

On 7 September 1921, James L. Chaffin died unexpectedly after a fall. Marshall, the third son, obtained probate without fuss; there was no reason for anyone to challenge the will, and there was no enmity or rivalry among Chaffin's children.

But in June 1925 the second son, James P. Chaffin, began having vivid dreams that his father was standing silently beside his bed. A week or so later the apparition,

23

dressed in the old black overcoat his son knew so well, spoke: 'You will find my will in my overcoat pocket.' James was convinced this was significant, and hurried to his mother's house.

His father's coat, however, had been given to her eldest son, John, who lived some 20 miles away. James went to John's home, and explained the situation. The two brothers examined the coat together. They found that the inside pocket had been stitched closed; when they cut it open, they found inside the rolled-up strip of paper in their father's handwriting. 'Read the 27th chapter of Genesis in my daddie's old Bible' was not a will, as James's dream had indicated, but the two brothers felt they must follow the message up.

John felt he could not look at the family Bible without independent witnesses, and took a neighbour, the neighbour's daughter, and his own wife and daughter with him. After a long search in his mother's house the old Bible was discovered in a top drawer in an upstairs room and, as it was being taken out, it fell into three pieces. The neighbour picked up the front section containing Genesis, and it opened automatically at the place indicated in the cryptic message. There lay the second will.

This will was tendered for probate in 1925. Marshall Chaffin had died a year after his father, but his widow contested the application on behalf of her young son.

The court assembled in December 1925 to decide the issue: the public areas were crowded at the prospect of seeing a classic family squabble burst into open view. The scandal-hungry locals were to be disappointed. On the advice of her lawyer, Marshall's widow withdrew her opposition when she saw the will itself, unmistakably in the old man's handwriting.

There are really only two stark alternatives in explaining this case. Either the Chaffin brothers were lying, and set up the whole elaborate hoax in order to lay their hands on their share of their father's estate, or the story is true from start to finish. But

Borley Rectory, dubbed 'the most haunted house in England', showing the gates at which a ghostly nun was allegedly seen. The dubious nature of the phenomena at Borley has led many to wonder since if the legend of the house lingers on.

the business of the Chaffin will is one of the best-documented and best-attested cases in ghost lore; and as such it stands as reasonable proof that in some cases, at least, ghosts do represent the consciousness of the dead – and that the physically dead do survive in some form of afterlife.

LOVE OF ADVENTURE

Some famous hauntings, however, leave one wondering to what extent some ghosts are purely subjective entities, existing solely in the mind of the witness.

Captain Joshua Slocum, the great American sailor, had a remarkable experience in July 1895, while on his historic solo voyage around the world in his sloop *Spray*. In the Atlantic, between the Azores and Gibraltar, he ran into squally weather. At the same time he began to suffer an attack of severe stomach cramps. These so distracted him that he went below – without taking in sail as he should have done. He threw himself on the floor of the boat's cabin, in great pain. In his account of the voyage he described what happened next:

'How long I lay there I could not tell, for I became delirious. When I came to, as I thought, from my swoon, I realized that the sloop was plunging into a heavy sea, and looking out of the companionway, to my amazement I saw a tall man at the helm. His rigid hand, grasping the spokes of the wheel, held them as in a vice. One may imagine my astonishment. His rig was that of a foreign sailor, and the large red cap he wore was cockbilled over his left ear, and all was set off with shaggy black whiskers. He would have been taken for a pirate in any part of the world. While I gazed upon his threatening aspect I forgot the storm, and wondered if he had come to cut my throat. This he seemed to divine.

'"Senõr," said he, doffing his cap, "I have come to do you no harm." And a smile, the faintest in the world, but still a smile, played on his face, which seemed not unkind when he spoke. "I am one of Columbus's crew, the pilot of the *Pinta*, come to aid you. Lie quiet, senor captain, and I will guide your ship while you have a calentura [a reference to the stomach cramps] but you will be all right tomorrow… You did wrong to mix cheese with plums…"

'I thought what a very devil he was to carry sail. Again, as if he read my mind, he exclaimed, "Yonder is the *Pinta* ahead, we must overtake her. Give her sail, give her sail!"'

Next day Slocum found that the *Spray* was still on the same heading as he had left her when he staggered below in his 'swoon'.

'Columbus himself could not have held her more exactly on her course,' he wrote. 'I felt grateful to the old pilot, but I marvelled some that he had not taken in the jib. I was getting much better now, but was very weak.. .I fell asleep. Then who should visit me but my old friend of the night before, this time, of course, in a dream. "You did well last night to take my advice," said he, "and if you would, I should like to be with you often on the voyage, for the love of adventure alone." He again doffed his cap, and disappeared as mysteriously as he came. I awoke with the feeling that I had been in the presence of a friend and a seaman of vast experience.'

Perhaps so. And perhaps, in his delirious state, Slocum imagined, or hallucinated, the whole thing. But if he did, another small miracle seems to have occurred: the *Spray* kept her course, with no one at the wheel, through a long bout of foul weather and a hostile sea.

'MERE' COINCIDENCE?

The best evidence that some ghosts present proof of a life after death comes from pacts made between friends or relatives in which each party promises that whichever dies first will 'come back' to the other to show that they still survive.

The best-known of these cases is that of Henry, Lord Brougham (1778–1868), the famous and fiery British reformer. Brougham made just such a pact with his old college friend Geoffrey Garner, one that eventually unravelled in a manner so hilarious that it has to be true. Some years after making this agreement, Brougham went travelling in Sweden with a group of friends.

'Arriving at a decent inn, we decided to stop for the night,' he recalled. 'I was glad to take advantage of a hot bath before I turned in, and here a most remarkable thing happened to me – so remarkable that I must tell the story from the beginning.

'After I left the [Edinburgh] High School, I went with Garner, my most intimate friend, to attend the classes in the University… We frequently discussed and speculated upon many grave subjects – among others, on the immortality of the soul, and on a future state. This question, and the possibility, I will not say of ghosts walking, but of the dead appearing to the living, were subjects of much speculation: and we actually committed the folly of drawing up an agreement, written in our blood, to the effect that whichever of us died the first should appear to the other, and thus solve any doubts we had entertained of the "life after death".

'After we had finished our classes at the college, Garner went to India, having got an appointment there in the Civil Service. He seldom wrote to me, and after a lapse of a few years I had almost forgotten him; moreover, his family having little connection with Edinburgh, I seldom saw or heard anything, and I had nearly forgotten his existence.

'I had taken a warm bath, and while lying in it and enjoying the comfort of the heat, after the late freezing I had undergone, I turned my head round, looking toward the chair on which I had deposited my clothes, as I was about to get out of the bath. On the chair sat Garner, looking calmly at me.

'How I got out of the bath I know not, but on recovering my senses I found myself sprawling on the floor. The apparition, or whatever it was, that had taken the likeness of Garner, had disappeared.'

On his return to Edinburgh after this farcical episode, Brougham learned that Garner had died in India on 19 December, the precise date of the apparition. Many years after the event, Brougham tended to be sceptical about it:

'Singular coincidence! Yet when one reflects on the vast numbers of dreams which night after night pass through our brains, the number of coincidences between the vision and the event are perhaps fewer and less remarkable than a fair calculation of chances would warrant us to expect. I believe every such seeming miracle is, like every ghost story, capable of explanation.'

Others, too, have suggested these cases are the result of 'mere' coincidence. But in their monumental collection *Phantasms of the Living*, published in 1886, the Society for Psychical Research described nine examples of an apparition following a pact of this kind. It is surely stretching scepticism to breaking point to suggest that all these apparitions are purely 'coincidental' with the death of the parties concerned, especially when such a pact is involved. And even if they are, the sceptics still cannot satisfactorily explain what those phantasms are or where they come from.

Nevertheless, it is clear from the apparitions and spectres we have discussed in this chapter that ghost stories, however well documented and however fascinating they may be, do not make the best or most consistent evidence for life after death. That evidence comes in subtler and, often, even stranger forms.

ANOTHER TIME, ANOTHER PLACE

The ancient Celts were terrible in battle as they had no fear of death – they would even lend money on the understanding that if it were not repaid in this life, it would be in the next. What made them so sure that this was not the only life?

The idea that the soul may journey through time, using successive human bodies as vehicles for the journey and the lives of those personalities it adopts as food for its spiritual journey to perfection, is foreign to Western thought. Judaism, Christianity and Islam differ widely in their notions of the kind of afterlife that awaits us, and of heaven and hell, but their broad message is the same.

'It is appointed for men to die once,' says St Paul in his epistle to the Hebrews, 'and after that comes judgement.' If we live in an upright, tolerant and kindly fashion, we shall be rewarded in the life to come – and if we do not, we shall be punished. The fundamental belief is that this is the only life each of us has, and that this life is the only chance we have to prove ourselves morally and spiritually.

So deep is this idea ingrained in Western thought that even in the increasingly irreligious 21th century it has actually proved possible to make money by gently mocking any idea of reincarnation at all. The New York journalist Don Marquis made a small fortune from regaling an eager public with the adventures of his characters Archie, the cockroach who had formerly been a *vers libre* poet but continued to write his versified diary by jumping up and down on the keys of a typewriter, and Mehitabel, the alley cat who 'once accused herself of being Cleopatra.'

However, belief in reincarnation is widespread, ancient and powerful, and the religions of some of the world's greatest civilizations have held that reincarnation may be combined with transmigration - the entry of the soul into the body of an animal. Such beliefs were common in the West before the rise of Christianity. One reason why the ancient Celts were so devastating as warriors was that they had absolutely no fear of death – so convinced were they of the reality of reincarnation and the continuity of their consciousness. They would even lend

31

money on the understanding that if it could not be repaid in this life, it surely would be in a future one.

DEATH AND BIRTH

In ancient Greece, belief in reincarnation was not incompatible with belief in the orthodox pantheon of gods. The Orphic sect, which flourished about 100 years before the golden age of Athens, had a view of earthly life that for gloom and self-punishment matched that of the most zealous medieval Christian flagellator. The Orphics called human existence a 'sorrowful weary wheel', and the only way to escape it was to live with the utmost self-denial and asceticism. Even then, only after many physical deaths and rebirths in both animal and human form would the soul be free.

The belief in reincarnation as such in ancient Greece was not confined to such killjoy cults, however. The mathematical genius Pythagoras, who lived around 500 BC, claimed to know that in former lives he had been variously a fisherman, a peasant, a shopkeeper's wife and a (female) prostitute. Pythagoras, it is true, also held fast to many quite eccentric beliefs, including some concerning the certain fearsome consequences of eating beans.

But Plato, one of the most profoundly original minds of the ancient world, was convinced of the truth of reincarnation. He held that the soul chose its new life at the moment of death, and might enter one of nine levels of being. Plato believed that this was not an endless cycle, and the soul was neither eternal nor did it necessarily progress, or even learn, spiritually from one life to another. Progress could be made if a soul chose its next life wisely, but Plato held that in creating a new physical body for its next life, the soul expended energy. Once its energy was finally consumed, the soul itself died out.

The Roman notion of reincarnation was somewhat different; the 1st-century AD political thinker Sallust, for example, maintained that children born with handicaps were bearing punishments for evils they had committed in former lives.

The other great ancient culture that firmly believed in reincarnation was Egypt. At first, the Egyptian religions held that only 'great souls', destined to lead mankind, were born again, but this belief gradually relaxed and expanded to include everyone from the highest to the lowest social classes. By the time the Book of the Dead came to be compiled, matters had, become distinctly formalized. The book contains incantations that would free the soul from its earthly prison in the tomb and prepare it for reincarnation. And it might come back as a plant – a lotus, say, or a sycamore – or as an animal; after 3,000 years of such transmigrations it would be ready to be reborn as a human being once again.

RETURN OF THE GODS

Christianity gradually expunged such ideas as it spread west from the Middle East, and seven centuries later Islam suppressed them as it began to spread south and east. But in places where these religions have arrived only within the last few centuries, native faiths continue to hold fast in their belief in reincarnation.

Throughout the Pacific, for instance, reincarnation is a bulwark of most native religions. The religions of many American Indian tribes endorse reincarnation, too. It has even been suggested that one reason why the 16th-century Spanish conquistadores found it so easy to conquer huge tracts of South and Central America, despite the existence of highly developed civilizations there, was the prevailing local belief in reincarnation. The Spanish leaders were seen as reborn,

A wealthy household in ancient Athens. The Greeks, for all their famous rationalism and philosophy, believed both in a pantheon of gods notorious for uproarious behaviour, and in personal reincarnation.

returning gods: in Mexico as Quetzalcoatl, and in Peru as Virochas. The Spanish lost no time in taking advantage of this 'heathen' error, and laid the country waste.

In Alaska, where gold and oil rushes have had more effect on local culture than any missionaries, the indigenous Tlingit people have retained to this day a powerful reverence for reincarnation, which they regard as a direct and immediate continuity from one life to another. Tlingit women pay careful heed to their dreams when they are pregnant, for it is then, in dreams, that a previously incarnated but now disembodied soul announces its intention to them to be reborn in the body of the new baby. At birth, diviners take great care to ascertain whose soul has been reborn, and then the baby is given the tribal name of the person it had been before. The child then takes credit for the good deeds done by its predecessors – but also has a powerful moral example that it must live up to.

THE WHEEL OF REBIRTH

In India, attachment to the idea of reincarnation has never wavered since the Hindu religion took hold and, some 3,000 years ago, its sacred writings began to reflect a belief in rebirth and reincarnation. In the Bhagavad-Gita ('The Song of Krishna'), the warrior, hero and god Krishna explains that he is the eighth incarnation of the god Vishnu, saying to Arjuna: 'Both I and thou have passed through many births. Mine are known to me, but thou knowest not of thine.' Hindus call reincarnation samsara, 'the wheel of rebirth'.

For Hindus, the number of reincarnations one may go through is infinite (and may include transmigration to lower forms of life, or even into rocks and stones), for the purpose of them is to give the soul the opportunity to rid itself of the imperfections that inevitably afflict it from its creation. Between each incarnation the soul enjoys a period of rest, in which it ponders on its progress towards moksha, the Absolute, which is also perfection and liberation – from which, paradoxically, the soul first emerged.

To rid oneself of these congenital flaws requires turning one's back on the world and realizing one's best, true nature. At the same time karma, the law of cause and effect, is at work: in essence this means that good is rewarded and evil is punished, and what is good or evil for the soul is judged on deeds and effects, not (as in Western religions) on intentions. Thus the Upanishads say quite clearly, 'Those whose conduct has been evil will have an evil birth as a dog, a pig, or an untouchable outcast.'

Earthly life is regarded as a burden, and at the same time as an illusion, called maya. The opportunities that this ostensibly unworldly outlook, combined with the rigid Hindu caste system, have offered for the exploitation of the poor by the rich have been plentiful, and usually avidly grasped.

The Sphinx, with the Great Pyramid in the background. These monuments were part of the ancient Egyptians' massive and elaborate system of belief and ritual concerning the afterlife.

THE SEARCH FOR THE DALAI LAMA

This observable corruption of a high ideal may have contributed to the inspiration of Siddartha Gautama, born a Brahman, the highest Hindu caste, around 566 BC. He was the heir to the crown of the Sakya clan on the Ganges in India, and is now known universally as Buddha.

The legend says that as soon as he was born Buddha vowed to end birth, old age, suffering, and death – in short, to break the endless grip of earthly life upon the soul. By the age of 29 he had realized that all were inescapable, and eventually propounded his Four Truths: that existence is suffering, and suffering is inevitable; that suffering is caused by desire; that eliminating desire will rid one of suffering;, and that the right conduct – the Eightfold Path – will rid one of desire.

Central to these principles was the belief that the soul was not (as Hinduism taught) an individual and personal thing, which drove the cycle of reincarnation. Rather, reincarnation was fuelled by the ego, which was constantly changing from life to life, and was an illusion besides. Rid oneself of ego, therefore, and one would attain nirvana – which does not mean heaven or the absolute, but simply extinction. Buddhism thus rejects any connection between social caste and the condition of the soul, although successive rebirths are inevitable if one is to work off the burden of karma from previous existences. But this is a matter of purifying the life force, in redeeming the individual.

One of the most fascinating ways in which the Buddhist belief in rebirth has practical effect is in the search for a successor to the Dalai Lama, leader of Tibet's Buddhists, when he dies.

The Dalai Lama is regarded as the incarnation of Chenrezi, the Buddhist god of grace, and he has taken earthly form 14 times since 1391. Each time the Dalai Lama (the term means 'greatest teacher') dies, the lamas of Tibet have the task of finding his reincarnated form – a small child born after the death – who will then be brought up to take on the leadership of the Tibetan Buddhist community. When the 13th Dalai Lama died in 1933, it took the monks six years to find his successor.

The search involves sifting a variety of normal and paranormal clues: the lamas scrutinize astrological signs, visions, dreams and other omens to establish when they should start their quest. After the 13th Dalai Lama's death, the corpse itself offered one clue. It turned its head toward the north-east. Then, in the mausoleum where he was laid, a star-shaped fungus grew on the north-east wall. In the mail courtyard of the monastery housing the tomb, a dragon flower unexpectedly grew by the north-east wall.

The lamas decided that it was in this direction that they should begin their search. To help them came a vision in a dream granted to one of the monastery's monks. He saw a place sacred to Buddhists – the lake at Chos Khorgyal, in China, and also a house with carved gables and eaves painted blue. Near here, the lamas concluded, they would find the child they were seeking.

In 1937 a group of lamas and monks set off for China to find the house. Two years later, at the village of Takster, they found it. One of the high lamas in the party disguised himself as a servant and went into the house. He found inside a two-year-old boy, Tenzin Gyatso, who instantly demanded the rosary that, beneath his disguise, the lama was wearing around his neck. This was not the lama's – but it had belonged to the Dalai Lama. Tenzin Gyatso then identified – or recognized – other rosaries, a drum and a walking-stick that had also belonged to the former Dalai Lama.

Encouraged by these initial signs, the lamas went on to look for physical confirmation that the boy was the current embodiment of Chenrezi. The various bodily characteristics, moles and birthmarks found on every Dalai Lama were indeed in place, and the lamas set about making arrangements for the boy and his family to travel to Tibet. Among these was paying a $300,000 ransom to the provincial governor for allowing Tenzin Gyatso to leave China, but eventually the infant Dalai Lama was installed in the Potala Palace above Lhasa to begin his long and arduous training to become the spiritual and temporal leader of the Tibetan nation.

The alleged reincarnation of the Tibetan Dalai Lama is not, in itself, proof of the reality of repeated rebirth. Without casting doubt on the sincerity of those involved, one could if one wanted pick holes in a number of aspects even in this one case. And the key to the matter, here, is profound religious belief;

Constantine, Emperor of Rome early in the 4th century AD. According to testimony given under hypnosis by Welsh housewife Jane Evans, she had once lived as the wife of Constantine's tutor during his residence in Britain.

driven by that, a sceptic would assert, the law of averages says that sooner or later the lamas are bound to find a suitable child to proclaim as their reincarnated leader.

On the other hand, there are many cases from the West, where there is no established traditional belief in reincarnation or rebirth, of people who, to their own surprise, have discovered that they have apparently lived more than one life on Earth.

THE SECRET MEMORY

The evidence for these claims has been gathered exclusively from hypnotic regression – that is, from subjects who have been hypnotized and then led back into the past to recall what they can of any former lives. Unfortunately, the most plausible of these – notably the alleged reincarnation of the Irish woman Bridey Murphy (1798–1864, according to the account given under hypnosis) as Wisconsin housewife Virginia Tighe (born in 1923), and the various lives recounted by Welsh housewife Jane Evans – have fallen apart in the light of detailed research.

Of these, the claims of Jane Evans were the most transparent. Once researcher Melvin Harris had burrowed into them, they looked more like a highly aerated Swiss cheese than evidence for reincarnation.

Jane Evans produced an astonishing wealth of detail about (for instance) life as the wife of the tutor to the young Constantine (later to be Emperor of Rome) in 4th-century Britain, or as a young Jewess caught up in the massacre of the Jews in York in 1190. This latter account in fact contained a wealth of thoroughly inaccurate information both about York and about the Jews of the 12th century, and most of it seems to have come from a play broadcast on BBC radio.

Jane Evans's life as 'Livonia' in 4th-century Roman Britain was taken almost word for word from a novel called *The Living Wood* by Louis de Wohl. It seems that Jane Evans had, quite honestly, forgotten that she had ever read any of the books on which her 'former lives' were based, but retrieved her memories of them from her subconscious while in a hypnotic trance. This phenomenon, known as cryptomnesia (from the Greek for 'secret memory') is familiar to hypnotherapists, and has indeed proved useful in digging out facts – often traumatic – about their subjects' early lives that they have often deliberately forgotten.

Another detailed recall of an actual historical event was provided by a subject known only as 'Jan' when she was put into trance by hypnotist Joe Keeton. Jan became 18-year-old Joan Waterhouse who, she said, was tried for witchcraft at Chelmsford Assizes, Essex, in 1556. All the details were proven to be historically correct – including the existence of Joan

Waterhouse and her presence in the dock. The only original source for Jan's – or Joan's – account that survived in the 20th century was a contemporary pamphlet, and the only surviving copy was in the library of the Archbishop of Canterbury's London residence, Lambeth Palace. Jan swore that she had never been there and had never seen the document.

But there was one bizarre anomaly. As Joan, Jan insisted that she had been tried in the reign of Queen Elizabeth I. Unfortunately, the English monarch in 1556 was Queen Mary I; Elizabeth did not accede to the throne until 1558. Given the ferment in religious life at the time, the supreme importance of the monarch in deciding and directing what religious practices were acceptable, and the sensitivity to such matters of people at the local level and their readiness to act in their own obsessive interests, this seems an extraordinary confusion.

And, indeed, there was an extraordinary confusion – in the mind of Joe Keeton and his subject 'Jan' – about what constitutes proper research. For the Lambeth Palace pamphlet had been reprinted during the 19th century, its solid black-letter type substituted by a fair attempt to reproduce a more legible typeface and design of Shakespeare's time. But there was one crucial error. The 19th-century printer had set the date of the Chelmsford witchcraft trial as 1556 – the date insisted upon by Jan and Joan. But the original plainly reads 1566 – by which time Queen Elizabeth had been on the throne for eight somewhat tempestuous years.

The only logical conclusion is that Jan had not, as she and Joe Keeton thought, once existed as Joan Waterhouse, accused of witchcraft, but had read, absorbed and – to be charitable – forgotten the reprint of the 16th-century trials at Chelmsford. But Keeton did not do this fundamental piece of research: a sceptic had to do it, and so debunk the case.

Perhaps the final word on hypnosis and progressive

reincarnation should go to a travel courier who, in the late 1980s, was accompanying a group of middle-aged American ladies on the Nile steamer from Port Said to Luxor. In the middle of a conversation about the politics of the Middle East, she said to this author: 'You think you got problems? I've got nine Cleopatras on this tour with me. You try keeping them from fighting.'

A MATTER OF FAITH

Is there, then, any real evidence for reincarnation?

Actually, and sadly for those of us who would like to have another crack at life in the hope that we might not make the same terrible mistakes again, the answer is most likely a resounding 'No'.

Some of the most apparently convincing evidence for re-incarnation has come from the researches of Dr Ian Stevenson, professor of psychology at the University of Virginia. Dr Stevenson has travelled the world, conducted innumerable in-depth interviews, and assiduously researched and reported a huge collection of cases that are, in his cautious words, 'suggestive of reincarnation'.

The British historian Ian Wilson has noted a number of problematic inconsistencies in Stevenson's evidence, and has also pointed out two particular but telling consistencies.

First, Stevenson has had to rely, during his extensive travels, on interpreters who generally already shared a belief in reincarnation with those he was interviewing. In some cultures people will tend to tell foreign visitors what they think the stranger wants to hear rather than the precise truth as they know it.

Second, Wilson has completed a careful analysis of the social backgrounds of the children claiming to have been reincarnated and compared them with the families of the people they allegedly once were. In an astonishing preponderance of cases, the family that the 'reincarnated' child has claimed to belong to has been of higher social status – from anything to an artisan (as opposed to a peasant) to a millionaire (as opposed to – a peasant). In a society in which belief in reincarnation is basic, and that is also circumscribed by a class system that is deeply underwritten by religious orthodoxy, any evidence that offers escape from certain wretched individual circumstances will surely be grasped at the earliest opportunity. Wilson does not say so directly, but it is not difficult to suspect from his evidence that the families involved in the claims Dr Stevenson has investigated have perhaps coached the children in question.

The truth or otherwise of reincarnation, then, has to remain, for the time being at least, a matter of faith. This does not mean that reincarnation does not occur – perhaps only for some people and not for others – but it does mean that there is no conclusive evidence for it at the moment. It is still an attractive idea. And it remains a bulwark of many ancient and respected cultures around the world.

An engraving from Zucchero's portrait of Queen Elizabeth I of England. The date of her accession to the throne, 1558, was the key to revealing the alleged reincarnation of the Cheltenham witch Joan Waterhouse.

THE MOVING HAND

The lady was ashamed of what had happened in the second-class compartment of the express train, and had intended to tell no one about her unpleasant experience. The famous journalist uncovered her guilty secret in a most unexpected manner…

The great 19th-century British journalist William T. Stead, the founder of the *Review of Reviews*, was also a spiritualist. Appropriately enough for a professional writer, he was also adept at automatic writing – which he used as a vehicle for telepathic communication with a certain lady friend. As proof of its efficacy, he recounted the following incident:

'[My friend] was to lunch with me on the Wednesday if she had returned to town. On the Monday afternoon I wished to know about this, so taking up my pen I asked the lady mentally if she had returned home. My hand wrote as follows:

"'I am sorry to say that I have had the most unpleasant experience, which I am almost ashamed to tell you. I left Haslemere at 2.27 p.m. in a second-class compartment in which there were two women and a man. At Godalming the women got out and I was left alone with the man.

"'He came over and sat by me. I was alarmed and pushed him away. He would not move, however, and tried to kiss me. I was furious and there was a struggle, during which I seized his umbrella and struck him with it repeatedly, but it broke, and I was afraid I would get the worst of it, when the train stopped some distance from Guildford. The man took fright, left me before the train reached the station, jumped out and took to his heels. I was extremely agitated, but I kept the umbrella.'"

Stead immediately wrote to his friend to commiserate, and explained how he had come by the information. He also asked her to call on him, and bring the broken umbrella with her. She wrote back, slightly disturbed that she had, apparently unconsciously, communicated the details of this event to him: she had intended not to mention it to anyone. She added that there was one incorrect detail in the account his automatic writing had produced – the umbrella had been her own, not her assailant's.

Author Alex Haley discovered when helping Malcolm X to write his autobiography that the Black Muslim leader habitually committed his unconscious thoughts to paper.

THE HAND THAT BETRAYS

This is an unusual case of communication by automatic writing, if not indeed a unique one, in that the person generating the message was alive at the time. Communication by automatic writing is usually thought of as the preserve of the dead.

In itself, automatic writing is not paranormal. Alex Haley, who assisted with the autobiography of the Black Muslim and political activist, Malcolm X, noted very early in their collaboration that 'while Malcolm X was talking, he often simultaneously scribbled with his red-ink ballpoint pen on any handy paper... I began leaving two white paper napkins by him every time I served him more coffee [which he drank in enormous quantities], and the ruse worked...'

Haley admitted that the projected autobiography 'got off to a very poor start', but by reading Malcolm X's scribblings (which, Haley said, 'documented how he could be talking about one thing and thinking of something else'), he was able to latch on to Malcolm X's real interests at the time, and steer their discussions so that the Black Muslim leader finally abandoned his reserve. Through these scraps of automatic writing, too, Haley was able to tell Malcolm X's true reactions to current events in his life – which were often quite different from what he would be saying publicly and to Haley. When he was officially silenced by the leader of the Black Muslims, for instance, he wrote: 'I was going downhill until he picked me up, but the more I think of it, we picked each other up.' Before he was assassinated, Malcolm X had set up his own rival mosque and militant black political organization.

The example of Malcolm X demonstrates clearly what Dr Brian Inglis has remarked – that automatic writing is 'the outcome of a different level of consciousness' rather than anything intrinsically paranormal. But that level of consciousness has often proven to be one that is sensitive to paranormal information: whether it is received from other people through extrasensory perception or whether it 'tunes in' to entities on a quite different level of being – for instance, those who have died.

Sir Edward Marshall Hall, who received news of his brother's death through automatic writing, three weeks before official notification of his loss reached him.

DEAD CERTAINTIES

In *The Paranormal*, Dr Inglis cites two fascinating examples of automatic writing that seem to have come from dead people and that produced information that no one living could have known by any normal means.

Sir Edward Marshall Hall (1858–1927), reckoned the premier English barrister of his day, was staying with his sister; among the guests was her friend Miss K. Wingfield, who was adept in automatic writing. When she agreed to give a demonstration of her gift, Hall took a letter that he had had from South Africa the previous day, sealed it in a fresh envelope, handed it to Miss Wingfield and asked her where it came from. The immediate response was: 'The writer of that letter is dead.' After further questions the automatic writing answered the original question: the letter had come from South Africa. What Sir Edward had not told anyone present (not even his sister) was that it had in fact come from his brother, and had been posted three weeks previously. Three weeks after his visit to his sister's house, Sir Edward received another letter from South Africa – telling him that his brother was dead. He had died in his bed the day before the session with Miss Wingfield.

The English healer Matthew Manning found that, when he was a teenager, automatic writing helped divert whatever psychic energy was wreaking havoc in his parents' home through poltergeist attacks. On one occasion the Manning family decided to get in touch with the spirit of Manning's great-grandfather, Hayward Collins, who had been a racehorse owner. They asked if he could give them the winners at a race meeting scheduled for the following day. None of the family had read what horses were running then, and deliberately did not do so until the end of the next day's racing. They found that great-grandfather Collins – or his shade – had correctly 'named six horses, which turned out to be runners: two came in first, one second, and two third, which would have netted a good each-way profit, had money been put on them'.

Collins, later, also gave this message through automatic writing: 'Put your money on Red Rum which will come in first, and on Crisp which will come in second. The third will be a tight spot so leave well alone.' Red Rum won the race. Crisp was second. The third place, a photofinish, was won by a short nose.

THE GLASTONBURY QUEST

One of the most dramatic indications that automatic writing may genuinely come from entities in the world hereafter resulted in the uncovering of Glastonbury Abbey. In the process, the career of the archaeologist concerned was ruined.

From 1191 onward Glastonbury Abbey flourished, as pilgrims flocked to the site of King Arthur's tomb, which was – so the monks said – discovered that year. The Abbey had a long history: it had been founded early in the 5th century by St Patrick before his mission to Ireland, which began in AD 432. In 1539, however, the powers behind the English Reformation cast their eyes on Glastonbury. King Henry VIII's commissioners executed the abbot, Richard Whyting, confiscated the

Red Rum, named as a sure-fire winner in a race described through automatic writing by the shade of an English healer's long-dead great-grandfather.

Abbey's lands and wealth, and wrecked the building. Over the next four centuries its stones sank from sight under the encroaching loam and a tangle of weeds.

In 1907 the Abbey ruins were bought by the Church of England. By then the neglected, overgrown site had become an enigma. The Church appointed 43-year-old archaeologist and architect Frederick Bligh Bond to excavate it. Bond was recognized as one of the leading English experts on Gothic architecture and a past master at restoring medieval buildings. Unknown to his new employers, he was also a devotee of psychic studies.

Bond's brief included the task of locating two chapels whose whereabouts were by that time a complete mystery. They were the Loretto and the Edgar chapels, built by Richard Bere, the last abbot but one at Glastonbury. Bere had also revived and promoted the legend that Joseph of Arimathea, the uncle of Jesus of Nazareth, had visited Glastonbury twice – first with Jesus when he was a child, and later, after the crucifixion, bearing the Holy Grail – the vessel from which the disciples had drunk at the Last Supper.

Bond was faced with a big problem: he had insufficient funds for a full-scale dig, and breathing down his neck was a rival architect, officially appointed to preserve the ruins Bond found, but in reality deeply interested in finding them first, and taking credit for the fact. Bond decided to undertake what he politely called a 'psychological experiment' to aid him in a job whose success otherwise depended on guesswork. The experiment was, in fact, a direct appeal to the spirit world through automatic writing.

DISTINCTIVE HANDWRITING

In the afternoon of 7 November 1907, Bond and his friend John Alleyne Bartlett sat down at a plain wooden table in Bond's

Bristol office. They were about to make their first attempt to communicate with the dead.

Bartlett had had considerable experience with automatic writing. He held a pencil lightly over a sheet of blank paper, while Bond rested his fingers lightly on Bartlett's other hand. After a false start, the pencil traced an outline that Bond recognized as the plan of Glastonbury Abbey. Then, curiously, it added a rectangle at the eastern end, beyond the high altar. Asked for more detail, the pencil – or whatever entity was behind it – confirmed that this building was the Edgar Chapel. It had been built, the writing continued, by Abbot Bere; Abbot Whyting had made additions to it. The pencil also traced another chapel to the north of the main Abbey building.

Asked who was writing, the entity replied: 'Johnannes Bryant, monk and lapidator' (i.e. monk and stonemason). Four days later, they learned that he had died in 1533, and had been curator of the chapel during the reign of Henry VII, and that the monks were 'very eager' to communicate. Further sessions of automatic writing with Bartlett over the following months produced a mass of information about the original Abbey buildings. It all came ostensibly from a number of long-dead monks, each of whom had his own distinctive handwriting, faithfully reproduced by Bartlett's pencil.

When Bond finally started work at Glastonbury in May 1909, he was faced with a dilemma: either he could follow the information he had acquired through psychic means, or he could take the view that he and Bartlett had invented it all, and depend on his own luck and guesswork. But in a sense Bond had no choice: the leads provided by the 'dead monks' were as good as any intelligent guess he could make, and they might be just what they appeared to be. He staked his reputation on the monks, and started digging according to their advice.

THE COMPANY OF AVALON

Bond's workmen duly dug trenches at the east end of the visible ruins and discovered a huge wall, more than 30 ft long, whose existence no one had suspected. Further digging revealed the whole of what could only have been the remains of the lost Edgar Chapel, precisely where the monks – who were now calling themselves 'the Company of Avalon' and 'the watchers from the other side' – had said it was.

Bond found time and again that the monks' automatic writing was absolutely reliable. For example, they told him that the chapel roof had been painted in gold and crimson, and Bond's workers dug up arch mouldings with the red and gold paint still intact on them. The monks said the chapel windows were stained azure, and Bond found fragments of blue stained glass among the ruins – to his own surprise, since most glass of the period was stained white or gold. Still more unusual was the monks' claim that at the east end of the chapel was a door leading to the street. Most churches simply don't have doors behind the altar, but the Edgar Chapel, it turned out, did indeed. The monks even told Bond the precise dimensions of the chapel, although he was sceptical when he first read them, for they seemed enormous. But they were correct.

The 'Company of Avalon' produced a mass of other information that explained finds at the Abbey; but Bond could not reveal what he was sure were the facts without revealing his sources. One of the more mysterious finds, as far as conventionally available knowledge went, was the skeleton of a 7 ft tall man found buried – without a coffin – just outside the walls of the Abbey church on the south side of the nave. Stranger still, between the giant's legs was another human skull.

According to the Company of Avalon, the skeleton had belonged to a monk named Radulphus. He had come to

England in 1087, after the Norman invasion led by William the Conqueror. William had installed a Norman abbot, named Thurstan, at Glastonbury. Radulphus had been Thurstan's treasurer. Before the giant monk died at the extreme old age of 103, he had asked to be buried as near as possible to the church he loved. But what about the extra skull?

A curious tale attached to this, the shades of the monks informed Bond. Abbot Thurstan and his Norman monks were notoriously cruel to the Saxon monks who had had charge of Glastonbury before their arrival, and at one point incited, or engineered, the slaughter of a number of the Saxons by Norman soldiers. A local earl, Eawulf of Edgarley, had led a reprisal attack against the Normans. In the battle he came up against Radulphus – whom he managed to wound severely with his axe – and then Radulphus slew him. He was buried in the Abbey grounds. When, decades later, the brothers were digging Radulphus's grave, they came upon Eawulf's bones. By chance he had been buried at the same spot that was chosen for Radulphus. The former enemies had been joined in death, their bones mingling in the same plain grave.

Bond spent months poring over old manuscripts to uncover some surviving documentary evidence of what the 'watchers' had told him through automatic writing. There was no known record of Eawulf, no scholar of the period had heard of him. But at the end of this odyssey through the crumbling chronicles of Saxon and Norman England, Bond had established that there had indeed been an earldom of Edgarley in Somerset in the 9th century at least; the obvious inference – at least it was Bond's – was that this was an ancestor of the Eawulf whose story had been told him by the dead monks of Glastonbury.

A DOOMED MAN

For more than ten years Bond kept secret the source of his seemingly – and, in fact – uncanny ability to unearth the most surprising new facts about the Glastonbury site. His discretion was not the result of any lack of faith in what he and Barrett had been told – the times his scepticism had been confounded were too many for that. The problem was the Church of England, which had always been hostile to spiritualism. Bond, already surrounded by jealous colleagues and suffering from a reputation for a dictatorial, even cranky, style of managing the Glastonbury project, would be bound to suffer if he described his experiments with automatic writing – no matter how fruitful they had proved.

In the end, the strain of remaining silent grew too great, and he decided, fatefully, to go public with the truth. In 1918 he published *The Gate of Remembrance*, which detailed the whole saga of his communications with the 'watchers' through automatic writing since 1908. As soon as it went on sale, Bond was a doomed man as far as his professional life was concerned.

The budget for the Glastonbury dig was slashed. Bond was saddled with an unsympathetic co-director, whose job was, plainly enough, to keep him in line. A monstrous Church bureaucracy suddenly took a singularly obstructive interest in his work at Glastonbury. Toward the end of his direct association with the Abbey he was demoted to cataloguing his finds for a miserly stipend of £10 a month. In 1922 he received a letter that, in the scrupulously polite but utterly chilling language of officialdom, summarily fired him from even that lowly position. His career, all too literally, was now in ruins. Even the most scholarly of his books were banned from sale within the Abbey precincts. Bond spent much of the rest of his life in the USA, pursuing psychical research rather than archaeology. He died alone, impoverished and embittered, in 1945.

Do Bond's and Barrett's ventures into automatic writing constitute reasonable proof of survival of death? That is certainly what they seem to offer, but one of the many ironies in the way the Establishment treated Bond lies in the sobering fact that he himself came to believe that they did not. Bond himself maintained that he and Barrett had gained access not to the words of the dead but to a storehouse of buried – perhaps racial – memory. This was something akin to psychologist Carl J. Jung's notion of the 'collective unconscious', but one specific to England and the English and their peculiar myths and traditions. The gateway of remembrance was his own intuition, released to run free through the discipline and concentration of preparing for his experiments in automatic writing. The power of intuition, he wrote, 'from the depths of the subconscious mind... has evoked these images'.

Such an argument is appealing, but its attraction may be somewhat specious. Because 'intuition' is familiar to us all, and because so many of Jung's ideas have acquired a kind of veneer of truth because they have been successful in treating people in psychotherapy, many people feel more comfortable with this form of words as they seem to describe the inexplicable rather than proof of survival of death. In a rigidly secular age, it may even be that most people do not wish to survive after the death of their physical bodies: perhaps their worst fears will come true. Perhaps, even, they fear that they could not cope with their deepest yearnings coming true, either. But to argue that 'intuition' is a better explanation than straightforward communication with the dead, for what Bond and Barrett discovered, is merely to substitute one unknown for another.

Sometimes things really are as simple as they seem. The evidence from the 'Glastonbury scripts' for life after death is probably as good as any we will ever have. That is until we die.

RULING PASSION

Frederick Bligh Bond, curiously enough, was instrumental in a case of apparent communication with the dead that, in contrast, throws up almost every question possible about the nature of psychic communications with the hereafter – ones that do not, however, seem relevant in his own involvement with the former tenants of Glastonbury Abbey.

In 1963, three years after the author's death at the age of 92, an intriguing book titled *A Tudor Story* by an Anglican clergyman, a canon of Peterborough Cathedral named William Packenham-Walsh, was published. It was in essence the record of one man's obsession with a woman who had died 332 years before he was born: in short, Packenham-Walsh's passion for Anne Boleyn, the second wife of King Henry VIII of England, born in 1507 and executed, after Henry had successfully pressed rather dubious charges of high treason, which included claims of adultery with her own brother, who was executed with her, on 15 May 1536.

Packenham-Walsh's interest in Anne Boleyn had first been aroused when, as a missionary in China, he read a biography of the dead queen in 1917. By the time he returned to England, the cause of Anne Boleyn – 'a queen who has been much misunderstood' – had become a ruling passion in his life. In August 1921 he instigated the first of many sittings with mediums that supposedly put him indirectly in touch with the dead queen – and with her husband, who was as temperamental in death, it seems, as he ever was in real life.

A modern Italian medium, Anita, at work. Although normally right-handed, she uses her left hand to receive messages.

This first session, with a medium called Mrs Clegg, did not involve automatic writing, but it did produce a wealth of information, unknown to the canon until his own researches confirmed it, about Anne Boleyn. For the disinterested observer it also raised the most fundamental questions about the nature of Mrs Clegg's mediumship. This is not to imply that she was in any way a fraud or a charlatan, but to question whether she herself understood the real nature of her gift (a problem we shall meet again in discussing other mediums and their alleged communications with the dead). There are two reasons for waving this flag of warning.

In the first place, during the sitting, Packenham-Walsh was unable to restrain himself from telling Mrs Clegg the reason for his visit: she soon learned who her visiting 'spirit' was supposed to be, so breaking a cardinal rule of objective psychical research. In the second place (at a later sitting), the purported Anne Boleyn made a curious prediction. The canon, she said, would be 'offered a parish with the snowdrops' and would 'go to it with the daffodils'. Not long after this Packenham-Walsh was offered the living of Sulgrave, Northamptonshire. When he first visited the parish it was covered with snowdrops. When he took up residence there, daffodils were everywhere. The vicarage gardener, according to Packenham-Walsh, said he had never seen anything like it in 40 years' service in his craft.

Even assuming that Packenham-Walsh's account is accurate and uncoloured by his deep desire to prove his particular point, and presuming a great deal of other things as well, there is no particular reason to infer from all this that Mrs Clegg actually was in contact with the shade of Anne Boleyn. She knew of Packenham-Walsh's interest and it seems much more likely that she was picking up information about the dead queen from Packenham-Walsh's own mind, and was dramatizing it as the word of the dead, than that she was in direct contact with Anne Boleyn herself. This is if anything borne out by the prediction that came true. Mrs Clegg was probably clairvoyant in a wide degree, but her understanding of her gifts had to be translated in terms of her spiritualist beliefs in survival after death. So, she was bound to present – just as Packenham-Walsh, for his own reasons, was bound to accept her precognition of the canon's future through the secondary medium of Anne Boleyn's allegedly discarnate soul.

SIMPLE DECEPTION

Frederick Bligh Bond became involved in Packenham-Walsh's psychical researches into Anne Boleyn because another medium, a Miss Eleanor Kelly, had received messages through automatic writing mentioning both himself and Bond. In due course, Bond introduced Packenham-Walsh, Miss Kelly had received messages through automatic writing concerning Anne Boleyn and Henry VIII, indicating their emotional states in the afterlife. Whether she knew of Packenham-Walsh's interest in Henry's second queen – in other words, whether she was guilty of drawing Packenham-Walsh to her through simple deception - Packenham-Walsh himself does not, of course, say. But the world of psychics is a small one, now as then. News, which cynics would call news of opportunities, travels fast.

On the other hand, if Miss Kelly's interest was genuine and disinterestedly concerned, and if these communications were equally genuine, it remains as likely that clairvoyance was responsible for the initial messages as for the later ones received in sittings with the canon. For nothing in the later messages revealed anything that Packenham-Walsh himself may not have concluded from his, by then, encyclopedic reading on the subject of the Tudor king and his tragically misused and betrayed second wife.

The basic matter of these sittings boiled down to the apparent fact that Henry was still locked in his ego – 'stuck', as modern psychobabble has it – and was busy either justifying his earthly actions or roundly abusing his 20th-century interlocutors. Anne Boleyn, not surprisingly, approved the canon's record of these proceedings as 'one of the ladders… by which many may climb to true knowledge'. By June 1924 – this time with two other and different mediums – King Henry was wanting it known that he had repented of his misdeeds. Few things can have been more musical to the ears of William Packenham- Walsh, but even by his own account few desires can have been less secret than his to rescue Anne Boleyn's reputation or to know that Henry had admitted how dreadfully he had used her.

Automatic writing, as such, then, is as ambiguous as any other means of communication in establishing the reality of life after death. But the experience of Frederick Bligh Bond remains to tantalize us with its implication that sometimes, somehow, we really can get in touch with those who have died – but who live on elsewhere.

GIFTS FROM THE OTHER SIDE

The investigator had checked for any sign of trickery and was convinced that the spiritualist was concealing nothing. Then, as he watched in astonishment, a fresh carnation materialized and began to fall from the medium's lips…

The late Anita Gregory was a distinguished scholar, a stalwart of the Society for Psychical Research in Britain, and by no means gullible when it came to paranormal matters – she spent considerable energy on showing how weak she believed the evidence was that anything truly strange had happened in the famous Enfield poltergeist case, for example. But at a seance held by medium Paul McElhoney in London in the early 1980s, Mrs Gregory was astonished and baffled when a small, metal model of Cologne cathedral landed in the palm of her hand 'from nowhere'.

McElhoney's spirit control, which called itself Ceros, explained through McElhoney that the model was a gift to Mrs Gregory from her dead father. At the time, this made little sense to her. Only later did she discover that her father and mother had spent their honeymoon in a hotel that looked out on to Cologne cathedral.

Paul McElhoney was a relatively rare phenomenon himself for the late 20th century: a spiritualist medium who produced physical phenomena. His peculiar talent was to produce objects, as Mrs Gregory so plainly put it, apparently 'from nowhere' – otherwise known as apports. His speciality was to bring forth flowers, often from his mouth; however he managed this feat, there was no doubt among the witnesses that they were all fresh. Unlike many other mediums, McElhoney would do this as often in good light as in the more traditional – and for sceptics, more suspicious – circumstances of a darkened seance room.

In November 1981, Michael Cleary reported in *Psychic News* how – through a relieving spiritualist — he had carefully searched both Paul McElhoney's person and his seance room for any sign of trickery before 'Ceros' had come through and entranced the medium.

Cleary noted: 'When Ceros brought the first flowers, the lights were on. I looked into Paul's mouth. There was nothing there then a flower began to fall from his mouth. Carnations are very significant in my Family. I had previously asked my mother in the spirit world to bring that kind of flower. When Ceros apported a carnation for me he said it was a present from a woman in the spirit world.'

SPIRIT GUIDES

It is a paradox of spiritualism that apports of material objects are regarded as proof of an immaterial life after death – immaterial, at least, as we understand the term. Mediums who produce such objects, and who create a wide variety of other physical effects during seances, are called, plainly and unsurprisingly enough, 'physical' mediums.

The hey day of the physical medium was the 19th century; spiritualism actually had its beginnings in the late 1840s in the most basic of physical-cum-spiritual phenomena – paranormal rappings that gave every sign of being intelligently controlled by someone, or something, who had survived death. Over the next two decades, mediums developed the ability to create an extraordinary repertoire of physical effects with the aid of spirits. (Mediums themselves would say, of course, that the spirits did this, and that they were indeed no more than the media through which these phenomena were produced.)

An outside observer would say that individual physical mediums tended to specialize in particular effects. A sceptic would say that that is because it is easier and better to perfect one kind of conjuring trick than to take on a number and suffer indifferent results. Mediums would reject both those ways of describing what happens, preferring to account for the difference between one and another medium's phenomena as the result of the predilections of their spirit guide, and as a matter outside their own personal control.

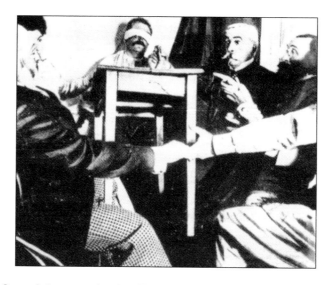

One of the most basic effects witnessed at seances in the 19th century and even today – the levitation of a table.

No medium claims to get directly in contact with a spirit on the 'other side'. It has become a convention, almost, among mediums, to have a 'guide' or 'control' – itself the spirit of a dead person but one seemingly more advanced than others – with whom they initially make contact, and who in turn mediates between the medium and the rest of the world of spirit. No one seems to have addressed the question of why this should be so (perhaps everyone has such a 'guardian angel' from the afterlife, but only mediums have the good fortune to be able to communicate with theirs). But mediums find that that is the way things are, and seem to have no difficulty in accepting it. Nor do they seem to balk at the remarkable number of American Indian medicine men or Zulus who seem to figure among spirit guides. That is the way things are. And if one wants to argue about the truth or falsehood of mediums, these are details; there are better and larger grounds for dealing with the truth of their claims.

'THE STUFF OF THE UNIVERSE'

Some mediums hear the voices of the dead; some communicate through automatic writing; some receive in the mind's eye photographic visions of pertinent material; and some produce physical phenomena which, they or the spirits believe, offer a concrete proof that spiritual life continues after physical death. The very fact that such phenomena are outside the bounds of normal physical possibility is deemed to be proof that only the spirits could have produced them.

Physical mediums have demonstrated an enormous range of such phenomena to prove their point. Among the effects that staid and reliable witnesses have reported are paranormal and apparently intelligently produced raps, as mentioned before; table tilting; disembodied voices speaking through 'trumpets' (essentially no more than paper or cardboard megaphones), or directly through the mediums themselves (a phemonenon closely related to modern 'channelling'); levitations of any number of objects from pieces of paper through pieces of furniture to the persons of those present at seances, witnesses as well as the mediums themselves; elongation of the medium's body; materializing detached and disembodied limbs; playing musical instruments that were well outside the reach of either medium or witnesses; and, most frequently of all in the 19th century, the production of that mysterious substance ectoplasm, which has been claimed to be the formative 'stuff of the Universe', the prototype of matter before it coalesces into recognizable physical form, from its original, allegedly spiritual state.

There have been reports too about individual mediums who have shown still more extraordinary capacities when under the influence of the spirits: they have been immune to the effects of fire, for example, or have produced materializations of their own spirit controls so real that those who saw them could not tell them apart from living flesh.

Here, we review a selection of the more interesting physical mediums from the great days of the seance room. If their manifestations were genuine then, according to them, so is the existence of an afterlife of some kind.

IMPERFECT HARMONY

Among mediums who produced apports, one of the most remarkable during the 19th century was undoubtedly Madame Elizabeth d'Esperance, actually a lady of English origin, whose more astonishing effects were produced through the spirit of a 15-year-old Arab girl named Yolande, who actually materialized as an entire physical form during Madame d'Esperance's seances.

At a seance held on 28 June 1890, this medium and the materialized Yolande produced a flower – not just any flower, or some sparkling cut hothouse bloom, but the seedling of a golden lily that in front of the astonished sitters grew before their eyes to a height of 7 ft, and in the process seven of the eleven flowers on the plant came into bloom and exuded a powerful scent. If this had been some species of vaudeville act, a professional conjuror would have made sure that the plant was either whisked away from prying eyes and sceptical inspection or equally 'magically' made to vanish. In this case, the spirit form of Yolande was disconcerted when she announced sadly that the giant lily could not remain in the material world, and then found that it refused to dematerialize.

Finally she told the sitters to keep the recalcitrant plant in a darkened room until they next met – a week later, on 5 July. The instructions were obeyed, and at the next seance the oversize

Ectoplasm pours from a medium's mouth. According to one unimpeachable source, its characteristic smell was of body odour.

lily was put squarely in the centre of the seance room at 9.23 p.m. Within seven minutes it had disappeared, but not before two of the flowers had been kept as mementoes of its brief existence and photographs had been taken of the massive plant in company with the medium.

Another reasonable proof, in the eyes of spiritualists, that the dead were able to communicate paranormally with the living was their apparent ability to play musical instruments without the assistance of any visible musician. Such phenomena were recorded from the earliest days of spiritualism. In the early 1850s, for instance, the Ohio farmer Jonathan Koons was, by his own account, instructed by the spirits to build a specially dedicated log cabin alongside his farmhouse in which to demonstrate his powers as the 'greatest medium on Earth', in company with his eight children.

The cabin was not the humble abode from which American country boys traditionally set out to crown their achievements with a spell in the White House. It was constructed like a miniature theatre, and had room for an audience of 30 people. Musical instruments were placed around the tiny auditorium. In this setting Koons and his children would take their places on a small stage. The lights would be put out, and Koons himself would take up his fiddle and play hymn tunes. Gradually, the spirits would take up the other instruments dotted about the room and join in – not, according to reports, always in perfect harmony. At the same time, a tambourine would be seen circling above the heads of the audience, trumpets floated into the air, and ghostly voices were heard speaking.

Koons did not make money from his bizarre presentations, and indeed actually encountered outright and aggressive hostility to his demonstrations from his neighbours. His motives seem to have been genuine and, in the light of the persecution he and his family received – the children were set upon, his fields and barns were attacked by arsonists, until in the end the Koonses left the district to become missionaries for spiritualism – it seems unreasonable to assume that the phenomena were not genuine too.

SPEAKING WITH MANY TONGUES

It's almost a commonplace today to see mediums 'channelling' the voices of the dead – reproducing the accents and idioms of the individuals coming through from the 'other side'. The seance rooms of 19th-century and early 20th-century Europe and America witnessed a similar phenomenon – but with a distinct and remarkable difference. For the 'direct voice' mediums who have emerged from time to time in the history of spiritualism have neither used their own voice-boxes to convey the words of the communicating spirits, nor have they been limited to being the channel for a single voice at a time. The voices, sometimes several at once, have come straight out of thin air to deliver their messages to the living.

New York medium George Valiantine demonstrated just such powers in 1924 in England. In seances held virtually every day over a period of five weeks, Valiantine was the medium for over 100 different voices. Numbers of them spoke simultaneously – and not only in English. The Welsh novelist Caradoc Evans held fluent, idiomatic conversations with his dead father in his native language (not an easy tongue to learn, with its difficult inflexions and unique system of mutations, and hardly one a New Yorker could mug up at short notice), while other spirits spoke with equal facility in German, Spanish and Russian.

The clinching demonstration of Valiantine's mediumship came in the late 1920s in New York. At a number of seances some voices that were frankly meaningless to the sitters had come through. On the off chance that he might be able to identify the language, the orientalist scholar Dr Neville Whymant, though sceptical of claims for the paranormal, agreed to attend a seance. He pricked up his ears and became strangely interested, however, when he heard a voice speak the name K'ung-fu-T'Zu – Confucius – in an impeccable Chinese intonation and accent.

Whymant responded by quoting a passage from the works of the ancient sage. This was more than a matter of finding out whether the shade of the long-dead philosopher would recognize his own work. Whymant was reasonably sure that the passage, though it made good sense, had been altered as it had been copied by generations of scribes. He had got no further than the first line when 'the words were taken out of my mouth, and the whole passage was recited in Chinese, exactly as it is recorded in the standard works of reference. After a pause of about 15 seconds the passage was... repeated, this time with certain alterations [that] gave it new meaning. "Thus read," said the voice, "does not its meaning become plain?"'

Whymant could hardly fail to be impressed. He reckoned there were perhaps half a dozen scholars in the West besides himself who knew enough Chinese – and were sufficiently familiar with the writings of Confucius – to have picked up his quotation with such ease, let alone subtly shifted the reading to give it a different sense. None of these learned men was in the USA at the time of the seance – and there was no question that any of them would have lent themselves to cheap trickery in the seance room.

A CURIOUS CHEAT

One of the more consistent exponents of physical mediumship in the 19th and early part of the 20th century was Eusapia Palladino. Born to peasant parents near Bari, Italy, in January 1854, Palladino made a name for herself as the focus of the most extraordinary physical manifestations during seances held in Naples. In 1891 the first of a series of tests and controlled observations, held all over Europe, were made of her powers by Cesare Lombroso, professor of psychiatry at the University of Turin.

Lombroso had had nothing but contempt for mediums, but came away from his encounters with Palladino remarking that he was ashamed to have disbelieved reports of what happened in spiritualist seances, adding, 'I am still opposed to the theory. But the facts exist, and I boast of being a slave to facts.'

The facts were indeed astonishing. Unlike the vast majority

of mediums at the time, Palladino did not insist on working under cover of darkness, and did not hide herself away in a 'cabinet' (a small chamber, rather like an enclosed pew, with a curtain across the front) as so many mediums did – often in order to hide the mechanics of their hoaxes. Palladino always allowed those present to tie her hands and feet if they wished, or take other precautions against her cheating. Another Italian scientist, Dr Ercole Chiaia, reported what he saw at her seances: 'Either bound to a seat, or firmly held by the hands… she attracts to her the articles of furniture which surround her, lifts them up, holds them suspended in the air… and makes them come down again, with undulatory movements, as if they were obeying her will. She increases their height or lessens it according to her pleasure. She raps or taps upon the walls, the ceiling, and the floor, with fine rhythm and cadence…

'This woman rises in the air, no matter what bands tie her down. She seems to lie upon the empty air, as on a couch, contrary to all the laws of gravity; she plays on musical instruments – organs, bells, tambourines – as if they had been touched by her hands or moved by the breath of invisible gnomes…'

The French astronomer Camille Flammarion reported that in one of her seances Palladino became irritable for some reason. As a result:

'The sofa came forward when she looked at it, then recoiled before her breath; all the instruments were thrown pell-mell upon the table; the tambourine rose almost to the height of the ceiling; the cushions took part in the sport, overturning everything on the table; [one of those present] was thrown from his chair. This item – a heavy dining-room chair of black walnut, with a stuffed seat – rose into the air, came up on the table with a great clatter, then pushed off.'

One of Palladino's most bizarre talents was to extrude, or somehow materialize, human limbs around her. On occasion she could produce entire human forms. In March 1902, one of the many scientists who investigated Palladino, Professor E. Morselli, had tied her carefully and thoroughly to a camp bed before a seance in which no less than six materialized forms appeared and disappeared. As each one vanished, Morselli checked the medium: he was still tied firmly to the bed.

One reason why Palladino was happy to be constrained in this somewhat undignified way was that she was, she freely admitted, incapable of controlling her actions when in trance. She claimed that in the presence of sceptics she would even react to their unconscious or conscious suggestions – and cheat. She was in fact caught cheating on at least two occasions: once during a visit to Cambridge, England, in 1895, and again in New York in 1910. This last occurrence ended her international career as a medium. But it is a curious kind of hoaxer who admits to her own propensity for fraud, and is caught only when a researcher deliberately lets go his guard to see what will happen – as was the case during the Cambridge series of tests administered by the Australian lawyer Richard Hodgson.

ENORMOUS REPERTOIRE

The greatest of the Victorian physical mediums was without doubt Daniel Dunglas Home, who impressed a huge range of witnesses from all walks of life from emperors to elevator attendants, who never took money for his seances, and who was never caught in any deception or hoax.

Home believed himself to be the illegitimate son of a member of the Douglas-Home family – better known as the Earls of Home – and he pronounced his name as they do, to rhyme with 'spume'. He was born in Scotland in 1833, but was brought up by an aunt in Connecticut, in the USA. In 1855 he was told by doctors that his consumptive lung condition would worsen if he remained in

America, and in the spring of that year he left for England.

Home had very little money, but he did have a wealth of psychic talent. He began giving seances when he was 17, after a classic spasm of poltergeist raps and hangings in his aunt's home had left him with powers of clairvoyance and healing. Within a very few years Home was to develop an enormous repertoire of bizarre and astonishing physical effects in the seance room.

In August 1852, Home levitated for the first time, at a sitting in the house of a Connecticut silk manufacturer, Ward Cheney. The editor of the *Hartford Times*, Frank L. Burr, described what happened:

'Suddenly, without any expectation on the part of the company, Home was taken up into the air. I had hold of his hand at the time and I felt his feet – they were lifted a foot from the floor... Again and again he was taken from the floor, and the third time he was carried to the ceiling of the apartment, with which his hands and feet came into gentle contact.'

Then, Home began to materialize disembodied hands. Burr told how one – 'very thin, very pale, and remarkably attenuated' – first took up a pencil and wrote. 'The hand afterwards came and shook hands with each one present. I felt it minutely,' he wrote. 'It was tolerably well and symmetrically made, though not perfect; and it was soft and slightly warm. IT ENDED AT THE WRIST.' Another chronicler of Home's feats described how one of these weird limbs picked up a handbell, rang it, and brought it to him. He tried to grab the hand: 'I had no sooner grasped it momentarily than it melted away, leaving my hand void, with only the bell in it.'

Home gave many demonstrations of such phenomena in London but, lacking an income, had to depend on the hospitality of his friends until 1858, when he married his first wife Alexandrina, one of the Czar of Russia's god-daughters. With this, material insecurity vanished, and his social standing instantly changed. Home was lionized by the most brilliant and

Daniel Douglas Home levitates himself above the heads of his astonished onlookers.

fashionable, as well as many of the weightiest intellectual members, of London society. The witnesses to his extraordinary powers thus included some of the least impressionable men and women of his day.

BIZARRE ABILITY

Home's seances were often held in good light, and he never hid inside a cabinet. He produced all the usual phenomena of the seance room: tables tilted or levitated (one, an occasional table with a single leg and claw feet, even managed to 'walk' up onto another table, 'exactly like a child trying to climb up a height'); an accordion that played by itself even when others held it in bemusement, watching the keys worked by invisible fingers; pens that wrote without visible assistance; materializations of human faces as well as his famous disembodied hands; raps and bangs; currents of air; and apports – among many others.

The Russian novelist and poet Count Alexey Tolstoy reported on the plethora of phenomena at a typical Home sitting, in a letter to his wife written in 1859. Besides the ringing bells, the levitations of furniture, the mysterious floating (and dissolving) hands, Tolstoy told how: 'The piano played with no one near it; a bracelet unclasped itself from the arm of Mrs Milner-Gibson, and fell on the table, where it lay surrounded by a luminous appearance. Home was raised from the ground... a cold wind passed round the circle very distinctly, and perfumes were wafted to us.'

But perhaps most striking of all his phenomena was not what Home did with other things, but what he did with his own body.

The levitations of Home, rising above the sitters – 'as if', as he put it himself, 'I were grasping the unseen power which slowly raises me from the floor' – were part of the standard Victorian medium's fare. One of Home's truly original effects was his quite bizarre ability both to elongate himself and to shrink. He normally stood about 5 ft 7 in tall. At one seance at the home of the art magazine editors Mr and Mrs S. C. Hall, a journalist – a hardbitten species of witness – reported that:

'Mr Home was seen by all of us to increase in height to the extent of some eight or ten inches, and then sank to some six or eight inches below his normal stature. Having returned to his usual height, he took Lord Adare and the Master of Lindsay, and placing one beside each post of the folding door, lay down on the floor, touching the feet of one with his head and the feet of the other with his feet. He was then again elongated, and pushed both Lord Adare and the Master of Lindsay backward along the floor with his head and feet as he was stretched out…'

Hall, measuring the distance between the two startled noblemen, found that a space of more than 7 ft now separated them.

A GREAT WIND RUSHING

Still more extraordinary was Home's relationship with fire. On one particularly memorable occasion he created a kind of parody of the Pentecost. Tongues of flame darted from his head and he spoke in some unknown foreign language while, according to Lord Adare, 'we all distinctly heard… a bird flying round the room, whistling and chirping. There then came the sound of a great wind rushing through the room…'

This was not all. Numerous witnesses testified how Home was able to handle live coals for minutes at a time without feeling any pain. The supremely eminent physicist William Crookes reported one instance:

'Home removed from the grate a red-hot piece [of coal] nearly as big as an orange, and putting it on his right hand, covered it with his left… and blew… until the lump of charcoal was nearly white hot, and then drew my attention to the lambent flame which was flickering over the coal and licking round his fingers.'

Was any of this proof of life after death? Home certainly believed so. He had been a committed spiritualist since 1850, when he saw a vision of his mother dying in Scotland; the mail brought confirmation later that this happened on the day of her death. She continued to appear to Home throughout his life, giving him useful and moral advice. But he believed that his psychic powers were the work of several spirits – the chief among them was called 'Bryan' – over whom he had no control. His work was spirit work. And no one ever caught him cheating.

CONVERSATIONS WITH THE DEAD

Lord Archibald turned down an invitation to visit his tenant farmer that fateful evening. The blood-curdling events of the night were to make him regret that decision…

One snowy winter's afternoon some time before 1885, Lord Archibald Zealand had been out with his wife, visiting their acquaintances. As their carriage rolled up the drive to Zealand Manor, Lord Archibald saw one of the tenant farmers on his estate coming away from the front door, having found his landlord not at home. Lord Archibald stopped to talk to the farmer for a while and, before he went, the farmer invited him to drop in at his farmhouse later that evening. Lord Archibald had a busy evening ahead of him, and turned the offer down.

Later that night, at about 10 p.m. Lord Archibald was in his breakfast room, working. He described what happened next to the editors of *Phantasms of the Living*, published by the Society for Psychical Research in London in 1886:

'I distinctly heard the front gate opened and shut again with a clap, and footsteps advancing at a run up the drive. When opposite the window, the steps changed from sharp and distinct on gravel to dull and less clear on the grass slip below the window, and at the same time I was conscious that someone or something stood close to me outside, only the thin shutter and a sheet of glass dividing us.

'I could hear the quick panting and laboured breathing of the messenger, or whatever it was, as if trying to recover breath before speaking. Had he been attracted by the light through the shutter?

'Suddenly, like a gunshot, inside, outside, and all around, there broke out the most appalling shriek – a prolonged wail… Of my [own] fright and horror I can say nothing – [but they] increased tenfold when I walked into the dining room and found my wife sitting quietly at her work close to the window, and in the same line and distant only ten or twelve feet from the corresponding window in the breakfast room. She had heard nothing.'

Too unnerved by this experience to go outside immediately to look for whatever had made this blood-curdling sound, Lord

Archibald waited till morning. No fresh snow fell in the night, but there were no signs of any footprints on the ground outside. Later that day, news came to the house that the tenant farmer Lord Archibald had spoken to the afternoon before had killed himself – apparently as the result of an unhappy love affair. He had ended his life by drinking prussic acid – and Lord Archibald's groom, who lived near the farm, had heard the man scream as he took the fatal dose and died.

The groom heard the dying man's cry at about 10 p.m. – 'as near as I can ascertain,' said Lord Archibald, 'at the exact time when I had been so alarmed at my own home'. The farm and the manor, however, were too distant from each other for him to have been able to hear the actual scream of the suicide. Lord Archibald's wife, after all, had heard nothing.

Surrounded by his family and a guard of honour,
John F. Kennedy goes to his last long home.

THE BANSHEE

Occurrences like this are known as cases of clairaudience – involving information that is passed on psychically through sound rather than through visual information. There are many cases of spontaneous, one-off clairaudience that, like the one above, occur only at moments of crisis and most often involve someone's death, but some people persistently and repeatedly hear information that they can only be receiving paranormally. And a few people claim to be able to hear the voices of the dead, speaking to them from the other side.

Among a number of old Irish families there is a tradition of clairaudience that is highly specialized, and not always welcome. This is otherwise known as the visitation of the banshee, which lets out a chilling howl as it announces the imminent death of a family member – though some say it comes to collect the departing soul.

The banshee is not only particular as to whose death it foretells; it is usually heard only by members of the family concerned. Irish tradition says that the banshee may also be seen – either in the form of an old hag or in the shape of a beautiful young woman – but reliable accounts of actually seeing the banshee are so rare as to be nonexistent. The term itself comes from the Irish *bean sidhe* - 'woman of the fairies' – but the notion that the banshee is female seems to have arisen from the sound of its voice.

That, by all accounts, is unmistakably feminine, though the sound of its cries ranges from the most wistful, gentle and seductive entreaties to the most spine-chilling and vengeful shrieks. The difference in the nature of these sounds apparently depends on the attitude of the banshee toward the dying individual and his family. That in turn depends on whose spirit the banshee represents, and how the family treated them in earthly life, for it is reckoned always to be the spirit of a long-dead member of the family concerned.

DEMENTED WOMAN

Tales of the banshee's howl are not confined to the misty Irish past. The banshee howled in the late 20th century as loud and clear as it ever did – and its eerie voice is by no means confined to Ireland. One Irish-American businessman from Boston, Massachusetts, who preferred to hide behind the pseudonym 'James O'Barry', told journalist Frank Smyth of three occasions on which he had heard the unearthly voice. The first time, when he was but a small boy, he was unaware even of the existence of anything called the banshee.

'I was lying in bed one morning when I heard a weird noise, like a demented woman crying,' said O'Barry. 'It was spring... I thought for a moment that a wind had sprung up, but a glance at the barely stirring trees told me that this was not so. I went down to breakfast and there was my father sitting at the kitchen table with tears in his eyes. I had never seen him weep before. My mother told me that they had just heard, by telephone, that my grandfather had died in New York. Although he was an old man he was as fit as a fiddle, and his death was unexpected.'

In 1946, O'Barry heard the banshee the second time, when his father died; he himself was in the Far East, serving with the US Army Air Force. He was woken up at 6 a.m. by 'a low howl': 'The noise got louder, rising and falling like an air raid siren.' On the third occasion, O'Barry was alone in Toronto, Canada, on a combined business trip and vacation. His account:

'I was in bed, reading the morning papers, when the dreadful noise was suddenly filling my ears. I thought of my wife, my young son, my two brothers and I thought: "Good God, don't let it be one of them." But for some reason I knew it wasn't.'

Indeed it was not. The time was just before noon, on 22 November 1963: the time that US President John F. Kennedy was assassinated in Houston, Texas. The president was a close friend of O'Barry's – and he was of Irish descent.

UNEARTHLY VOICES

As with other paranormal phenomena, there is nothing new about clairaudience. The ancient Greek philosopher Socrates was familiar with the promptings of what he called his 'daemon'. They were, he told his judges at his trial, 'constantly in the habit of opposing me even about trifles, if I were going to make some slip or error'. He had decided to stand trial for his life (albeit on somewhat frail charges) because his voices had not positively advised him to flee from Athens and, as he remarked to the court, he took this as a sign that 'those of us who think death is an evil are in error'.

Socrates, thus, seemed to think that his voices came from somewhere beyond this earthly life. In the Christian era Socrates would probably have been made a saint, and as such would have been in the company of two fascinating Christian women who, too, heard voices from unearthly realms.

One was Catherine of Siena (the Italian city where she was born in 1347). Catherine not only believed, like other mystics of her time, that among the voices she heard one came directly from God; she seems to have been actually clairvoyant, with the voices giving her information about ordinary human affairs. Some time after she had converted an aristocrat, Francesco Malevolti, to Christianity – and so taken him from a life of singular debauchery – the young man slid back into his former depraved existence. Catherine told him bluntly that she knew from her voices everything he did, and then recited to him a catalogue of his latest doings, sayings and sins. 'When I heard her tell me precisely all that I had done and said,' commented Malevolti, 'confused and shamed, and without an answer, at once and heedfully I fulfilled her command.'

DIVINELY INSPIRED

Possibly the most outstanding clairaudient in history was St Joan of Arc. Born in 1412 into a peasant family and illiterate all her life, Jean la Pucelle, 'the Maid of Orleans', first heard voices when she was only 13 years old. They told her that she could save her country from its enemies – France was then at war with England and the Duchy of Burgundy. Four years later, by sheer force of character, she persuaded the Dauphin (crown prince) of France to let her join the French army that was attempting to relieve the siege of Orleans by the English. She effectively took command of the army, and 10 days later the English were defeated.

Other victories followed, and Joan persuaded the Dauphin to be crowned as Charles VII of France. He, however, did not follow up the moral and military advantage Joan had created, and when she attempted to break another siege more or less alone, she was captured by the Burgundians, who sold her to the English. They tried her for witchcraft, and – conviction being a foregone conclusion – she was burned at the stake in Rouen in 1431, still not yet 20 years old.

Such a career would be astonishing enough, but it is all the more extraordinary that it was based on psychic ability. Joan's voices did not limit themselves to inspiring her to battle or to mystical utterances: they provided specific information. They directed her to the one man likely to introduce her to the Dauphin, for instance, and she impressed him less by her patriotic and religious fervour than by her ability to tell him, in a courtier's words, 'matters so secret and hidden that no mortal

*The ancient Greek philosopher Socrates, whose profound,
still-relevant thought was prompted not by deep meditation,
but by inner voices entirely outside of his control.*

except himself could know them save by divine revelation'.
These 'matters' had been revealed to her by her voices.

There are many other instances of the efficacy of Joan's
voices, from her – or their – accurate prediction (recorded a
fortnight before the event actually occurred) to the Dauphin that
she would be wounded by an arrow at the siege of Orleans, to
the information that there was a sword behind the altar in the
church of St Catherine at Fierbois. She wrote to the clergy in
Fierbois, telling them to look there; and they found a rusty sword.

Joan of Arc made no secret of her clairaudience, and it was this that condemned her in the eyes of the English court that tried her for witchcraft. As a later commentator put it, she died because of her 'resolute insistence on the truth of the very phenomena which were being used to destroy her'. Joan, naturally enough for anyone of her time, believed her voices were divinely inspired. To 21st-century eyes, she was a psychic, but there seems no doubt of her integrity or truthfulness concerning those voices and what they had to say, and little doubt either that they spoke with uncanny accuracy.

PHANTOM STEPS

Clairaudience, as these historical examples have shown, does not limit itself to precognition, telepathy – or to communication with the dead. Clairaudience is really the auditory awareness of all kinds of extra sensory perception, and only a portion of recorded instances of the phenomenon can be said to offer any evidence at all of life after death.

Socrates seems to have taken his voices as implying that life continued in some form after death, although he did not assume that they came from the realm of the dead itself. St Catherine of Siena and Joan of Arc certainly attributed their voices to spirits, but they were very particular spirits indeed – the Archangel Michael, for instance, was among them. And it was perhaps inevitable that these two women, of such profound and visionary Christian belief, should have identified their clairaudience with the hosts of God. To the medieval Christian there was only one alternative – they were the work of the Devil.

The most commonly reported clairaudient communications with the dead have actually occurred at the point of death.

Karl von Linne (1707–78), the Swedish botanist who established the modern system of classifying living things by

Latin names, was not so coldly scientific that he was immune to such events. His house in Uppsala contained a botanical museum, and one night in 1776 he and his wife were woken by loud footsteps pacing about the gallery. No one should have been there at all, since von Linne had locked the doors and, in fact, had the key with him. Then he recognized the footsteps as those of his closest friend, Karl Clerk, but he found neither Clerk nor anyone else in his museum. A few days later, he learned that his friend had died 'at precisely the same hour' as he had heard the phantom steps in his house.

A still surer indication that clairaudience acts as a channel between the living and the dead was recorded by Camille Flammarion in his 1922 book *Death and Its Mystery*.

In response to an appeal for such experiences, Flammarion had been told the story of a French girl named Clementine, who had suffered such a terrible life in the company of her alcoholic father that she decided to escape by entering a nunnery. Clementine's aunt gave her shelter when she first fled her father's house, but the older woman had a presentiment that Clementine did not have long to live. And she told the girl so.

Clementine seems to have had the same intuition, but made light of it. She knew she didn't have long to live, she said, but she would make sure her aunt knew when she died. 'I'll make an outrageous racket for you,' she promised.

Clementine in due course entered a convent, safe at last from the predations of her father. Some time after this, the aunt's entire household was disturbed one night around its usual bedtime by an 'outrageous racket' indeed. There were sounds from the roof as if it were caving in, and the very housebricks seemed to be slamming against one another. At the same time, there was no movement to be seen and no actual damage to the fabric of the house. Clementine's aunt guessed in a flash what had happened.

'Clementine is dead,' she said in a firm voice. At once, the uproar stopped as abruptly as it had begun. The next day, a telegram arrived at the house from the convent, breaking the news of Clementine's death – which had occurred at exactly the time that the clearly paranormal 'racket' had broken out.

UNCANNY VISIONS

By far the most renowned clairaudient of modern times was Doris Fisher Stokes, who for millions of people all over the world came to personify mediumship and contact with the next life. She was a natural star of television chat-shows and stage 'demonstrations' precisely because she was so natural – down to earth, unpretentious, unburdened by any New Age claptrap or desire to surround her talent with occult significance. Talking to the dead through Doris Stokes was an extraordinary experience just because she made it seem so everyday – and at the same time, she seemed hardly able to believe her own success.

In her early life she certainly had no reason to expect it. Doris Fisher Stokes was born the daughter of a blacksmith and a washerwoman, Tom and Jen Sutton, just after the end of World War One, in Grantham, Lincolnshire.

In World War Two Doris Stokes joined the Women's Royal Air Force and worked in operations rooms plotting the progress of Allied bombing raids on Europe. She found she had an uncanny and disconcerting foreknowledge of which aircraft would not return from their missions. It was only in 1944, after her husband John, a sergeant in the elite Parachute Regiment, failed to return (along with so many others) from the disastrous airborne assault on Arnhem in Holland, that Doris Stokes began to take either her own paranormal talent or evidence of survival after death very seriously.

At that time she had a vision of her father, who had died

when Doris was only 13 years old. He told her two things: that John was alive, though a prisoner of war, and that their new-born son would shortly die. Both proved true. After that, she began attending her local spiritualist church. Her sensitivity developed, and she was soon practising as a medium herself.

TALKING TO THE DEAD

Doris Stokes said that she had two means of knowing when a soul from 'the other side' wanted to communicate. Either her spirit control – an entity claiming to be a deceased Tibetan Lama called 'Ramonov' (which is not the form of any known Tibetan name) would tell her 'in her ear', or she would see a

Camille Flammarion, French astronomer and sometime president of the British Society for Psychical Research, among whose voluminous writings on psychic matters was an especially poignant case of clairaudience.

small blue light appear over the head of a sitter, which indicated that someone close to them was trying to 'come through'.

Doris Stokes captivated huge audiences and many individual sitters too. She did so because time and again she produced information from the 'other side' that could have been known only to the individual she was talking to on 'our side' and to her unseen communicators. Yet some odd doubts remain about whether she was in fact able to converse in the easy way she had with the dead.

Doris Stokes has been accused of fraud since her death. She admitted to cheating once or twice during her lifetime. But to offer some perspective on her mediumship, one has to give personal testimony.

The author of this book saw Doris Stokes in action three times: once at a private sitting in 1981, once at a press conference to launch one of her several books in 1982, and once (while on a flying visit to London) at a stage 'demonstration' in front of a packed house at the London Palladium late in 1985. The first two were highly impressive. The third was not, for reasons that will become clear.

The first occasion was as much a social one (in which I hoped to get some measure of Doris Stokes) as a formal 'sitting' as such. I was not the sitter (an old business colleague was) but over dinner before the sitting began, Doris Stokes made a number of casual observations about my life that were entirely accurate, although she had never met me before and as far as I know heard my name for the first time that evening. Two remarks in particular stand out: 'You've been a soldier, haven't you, love,' she said, 'and you don't know whether to be proud of what you've done or not, do you? But you don't talk about it.' All three of these statements were (and are) true.

Her second memorable remark concerned a ring I was wearing: 'That doesn't belong on that finger! You've moved that, haven't you, love?' The ring was on the little finger of my left hand. It was, in fact, my wedding ring. When my wife and I broke up, I moved it from the ring finger of my left hand to the pinkie, for a mass of tangled emotional reasons.

MIND READER?

The sitting itself was extraordinary for the wealth of detail that Doris Stokes produced about my colleague, some of which plainly embarrassed him because of my presence. But she told him nothing that he did not know already – nothing that he did not, then or later, confirm from his own knowledge. This is interesting because at about the same time the staff of the weekly magazine *The Unexplained* reported that they had invited Doris Stokes to a sitting that - reading between the lines – followed a curiously similar pattern. Settling on a young lady member of the staff whose grandmother had recently died, Doris Stokes found herself in communication with the old lady herself, but almost everything she had to communicate was already known to the girl.

No explicit conclusion was drawn from this significant fact in the magazine's report of the encounter, but in an assessment of the occasion written some years later, the editor of the magazine had this to say:

'When asked… whether she had considered the possibility that she was, in fact, reading the (unconscious) minds of her sitters, Doris Stokes replied that she would refuse to carry on her work if she felt she had been doing any such thing. "That would be an invasion of privacy," she said. "I don't think God would allow that." Nonetheless, the possibility remains that Doris Stokes is… highly telepathic, picking up memories from the mind of someone who knew the dead person [that is, of course, the sitter him- or herself). These memories are then dramatized by Mrs Stokes's own subconscious, and come to her in the form of voices…

'Presumably the reasons for this are two fold. In the first place, Doris Stokes has [a] very strong resistance to the notion that she is invading other people's most private space – the mind. And [in the second place]… she has been utterly convinced that we do survive death. She cannot prevent her talent manifesting itself, and so has rationalized it in a way that has brought her, and thousands of people who have sat with her, great comfort.'

SERIOUS QUESTION MARKS

This seems a very fair and logical deduction: Doris Stokes was not – as she undoubtedly, most sincerely, believed – in touch with the dead, but she was in touch with the minds of her sitters. But she was also, it seems, guilty of a quite different kind of touch – simple, basic fraud.

In *The After Death Experience*, published in 1987, author Ian Wilson described how he found out that Doris Stokes packed her public appearances with people (whom she placed in reserved seats at the front of the auditorium) whose personal details were, he and other researchers discovered, no secret to her. And the most impressive 'readings' at those appearances were, of course, for the people she had specially invited and with whose particular, intimate details she was already familiar.

Having attended such a demonstration – which followed exactly the pattern Wilson describes in his book – I can only agree with his conclusion: that at this stage in her career Doris Stokes was 'not all she seemed, and the most serious question marks hang over her'. In the same paragraph, Wilson generously suggests that Doris Stokes might 'really have been a genuine medium… rigging her shows through sheer fear of facing a huge audience' lest no 'other-worldly messages' came through. That is possible, but Wilson seems not to have taken one further factor into account.

When he saw Doris Stokes at the London Palladium – and discovered how she seemed so accurate in her readings – on 16 November 1986, Doris Stokes was dying of cancer, and she knew it. She actually 'passed over', as she would have put it, less than six months later, on 8 May 1987. The evidence that she rigged her last big public demonstrations is difficult to refute, but by then Doris Stokes had become part of show business – whose brave and tragic motto is 'The show must go on'. My own experience of Doris in less clouded and painful days suggests that she did have a genuine talent, and my experience of her later suggests that her last illness at least (there may have been other reasons) combined with a sad and mistaken sense of loyalty to her audience to override her own honesty and integrity.

The real question for students of the paranormal is whether, at the height of her power, Doris Stokes communicated with the dead, or simply made contact with the minds of her sitters. We know her own answer to that question. We do not know the real answer.

Doris Stokes takes a rest between sessions at a public demonstration in 1984. In the last few years before her death in May 1987 suspicions grew that her shows were not all that they seemed.

LIVING ART FROM
A DEAD HAND

The teenager took up psychic art in the hope of ridding his family home of the destructive poltergeist, but as his pen and paintbrush re-created the masterpieces of the great artists, he found the demands made on him both baffling and exhausting.

There are two kinds of 'psychic artist'. There are those whose paintings, drawings, writings or musical compositions are guided by long-dead artists. And there is a handful of visual artists who draw or paint portraits of those they see 'in spirit'. What kind of evidence does the work of these two quite different groups of artists offer for life after death?

To some extent the answer to the question depends on the art involved. In the early 1970s, the British healer Matthew Manning – then still a teenager – began what became a huge collection of paintings, drawings and sketches that were created 'through' him by artists as diverse as Leonardo da Vinci, Claude Monet, Aubrey Beardsley, Beatrix Potter, Paul Klee and Pablo Picasso. Manning did not go into trance to produce the pictures; he simply concentrated on the artist while sitting in front of a sketching block with pen, pencil or paintbrush at the ready.

In his book *The Link*, Manning admitted to being baffled by what was happening when he painted or drew these pictures. He commented: 'How do I ask Albrecht Dürer to draw through me... ?... The fact that the person I wish to communicate with does not speak English is apparently no barrier.'

Strangely, what did prove a problem for many of these long-gone artists was how to use colour (Picasso was a notable exception). But this difficulty, paradoxically enough, may be a sign that the communication between Manning and the artists was genuine.

One is reminded of the frustration expressed by psychical researcher Frederic W.H. Myers (through a medium's automatic writing) five years after his death in 1901: 'I appear to be standing behind a sheet of frosted glass – which blurs sight and deadens sounds – dictating feebly to a reluctant and somewhat obtuse secretary.' At least the problem shows that Manning, if not in trance, was not in his normal state of consciousness. A reasonably talented painter in his own right, he had won prizes for art while at school, and should not have had any difficulty in using colour if he had been in full conscious control of his materials.

PSYCHIC COLLABORATION

Some of the pictures produced like this were very close to those created by the artists in their lifetimes. Manning – or the Renaissance artist himself – made a remarkably accurate reproduction of a sketch of a hanged man by Leonardo. Another such 'copy' was of Beardsley's famous drawing of Salome. In themselves, of course, these pictures prove nothing at all about survival. Manning speculated on this point: 'The only explanation I have is that the artist appears to be making a point of identifying himself beyond a shadow of doubt by reproducing something with which he is already known to be associated.'

Beardsley, however, was apparently also prone to make mistakes and to change his mind – as any living artist might – when working through Manning. 'More than any other... Beardsley made many mistakes while drawing,' said Manning, 'but instead of covering them over with paper, which obviously he could not do, he inked over them and changed them into something different.'

These works were often finished very fast – most in an hour or two, and without any preliminary sketching – far quicker and more spontaneously than a working artist would expect to complete a picture. This did not make the process easy, however. Picasso was a particularly demanding taskmaster: 'No other communicator tires me out as much as Picasso does,' wrote Manning. 'After only a few minutes, the time it takes him to do one drawing, I feel worn out and cannot continue for at least 24 hours.'

Matthew Manning claimed to have had a special connection with Pablo Picasso.

The Manning collection of psychic art seems authentic enough: but was it really produced by artists in the afterlife, using Manning as a medium? In *The Link* Manning states clearly of his psychic collaboration with Picasso: 'The first work from him came in July 1973, three months after he died. I specifically asked Picasso to produce a drawing for me.' But an equally valid interpretation is that Manning was unconsciously trying out – or trying on – a number of identities through his artistic efforts. He took up 'psychic art' and automatic writing, after all, in the hope of channelling his own inner conflict into less destructive paths than the particularly unruly poltergeist that had plagued him and his family for some years.

Manning in fact later distanced himself as far as he could from the idea that he was in touch with the spirits of the dead. In the early 1980s, he said, 'I have never [sic] claimed my drawings to have been communications from the spirits of deceased artists… I feel that I was merely attuning myself to the continuing inspirational force created in the first place by the artist. That is why many of my drawings are only copies, sometimes not very good, of drawings already made by the artist.'

PROLIFIC OUTPUT

Such a statement, complete with its economy with the truth, amounts to recantation. Such qualms have never had to cross the mind of London medium Coral Polge, but she does not even pretend to be continuing the work of famous dead artists. Her speciality is drawing portraits of quite ordinary people who have died – and she draws them not from photographs, nor from any other kind of image, but from feeling their presence 'in spirit'.

'I know exactly what to draw,' she has said, 'without thinking about it. It's involuntary, like breathing or walking.'

Coral Polge did actually train as an artist, although ironically she was 'hopeless' at portraits as a student in the 1940s; in any case her real interest then was in textile designs. But she was interested in spiritualism, and became a medium herself in due course. When another medium suggested she had a future as a psychic artist, she responded first by producing portraits of the spirit guides – those in the afterlife who, according to spiritualists, act as individual 'guardian angels' for every one of us – of her sitters.

But many people (including Coral Polge) found these unsatisfactory, since they so frequently could not be identified easily from the historical records. They were often Red Indians, nuns, monks, Chinese sages or even Zulus, often from distant epochs. They were not the easiest people to track down in their earthly existences. Gradually she moved on to drawing portraits of the dead relatives, friends and loved ones of her sitters.

She cannot produce portraits of the dead on demand, however. 'It creates barriers when people come expecting or wanting me to draw someone in particular,' she has said. 'I draw whoever comes through.'

In doing that – without any visual stimulus at all – she has been both prolific and extraordinarily accurate. It has been

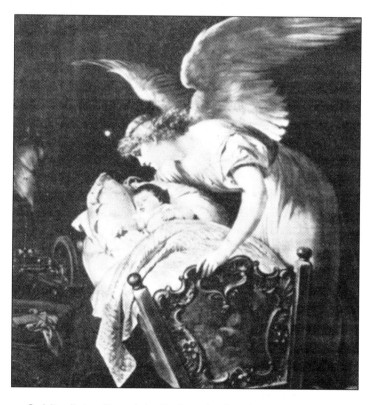

Spiritualists often claim that each of us has an individual guardian angel.

estimated that between 1950 and 1970 she drew nearly 1,800 portraits a year. Three out of the thousands of sittings that Coral Polge has taken over the years will show how precise her psychic vision can be.

AMAZING ACCURACY

One of her sitters was writing a book about the former UN Secretary-General Dag Hammarskjold, who had been killed in a mysterious aircraft crash in 1961. The visitor made no bones about her hope that Coral Polge would produce a portrait of the dead diplomat. Coral Polge did not feel able to oblige – as she says, such a demand 'creates barriers' – and her sitter was disappointed when Coral's pencil began to sketch the outline of what seemed to be a little girl with flowing blonde hair.

Coral's sitter in fact felt doubly disappointed, for she had been told by Hammarskjold through another medium that she would have a portrait of him from a psychic artist. At first it seemed that it was not to be this psychic artist – until Coral Polge had all but finished, and her sitter realized that she had drawn not a portrait of Hammarskjold as an adult statesman, but as a child. In Coral Polge's drawing she recognized Hammarskjold as she had seen him in a photograph taken when he was aged only two – complete with long fair locks, not unusual in small children in 1907.

Another had a double confirmation of Coral Polge's abilities as an all-round medium as well as psychic artist at a public meeting at which Coral was producing drawings as they came to her, and then asking the audience if any of them recognized the resulting portraits. Mrs Phyllis Timms, from Salisbury, Wiltshire, was sure that one such picture, showing an elderly man with a drooping, bushy white moustache, was of her late maternal grandfather, Herbert Light. No one else in the auditorium made any move to claim it.

But Mrs Timms wanted some further sign that the picture was indeed intended for her. Coral Polge, picking up some further psychic impression about the man she had drawn, suggested the portrait might be for someone in a green dress. Mrs Timms was wearing blue. Coral Polge insisted that green was the key link between the man in her portrait and someone in the here and now. It was only at this point that Mrs Timms stopped thinking about colours and realized the significance of the word 'green'. Her maiden name, which she had not used for years, was Green. She claimed the picture.

These cases could be 'explained' by suggesting that Coral Polge had picked up her knowledge of her subjects' looks from the sitters – for it was the sitters she depended on to recognize whose likeness she had drawn. But in some cases the connection between sitter and portrait is not as direct or clear as that, and only later has the accuracy of Coral Polge's drawing come to light.

Singers Grace Brooks and Deirdre Dehn met when they were both working on the film of Lionel Bart's *Oliver!* Deirdre, it turned out, had a talent for automatic writing. Through her scripts, another singer, who first identified herself as Maria Garcia, communicated with Grace. Later 'Maria' gave her surname as Malibran. Intrigued, Deirdre went to work to find out if this was indeed a historical person, and her research discovered that Maria Malibran had been born Maria Garcia in Paris in 1808. She made her debut as an opera singer in London in 1825, and died tragically at the age of 28 in Manchester, England, as the result of falling from a horse.

Maria Malibran was a real enough person, then. In due course, Deirdre Dehn went home to Australia, and that seemed to be the end of Grace Brooks's contact with Maria. Then she went to a sitting with Coral Polge. Coral drew a portrait of a young woman with a hairstyle that was definitely not in any modern style. All Coral Polge could tell Grace Brooks was that This is a Spanish singer named Maria.'

Grace Brooks had no idea what Maria Garcia Malibran looked like, but she did know how to find out. Research in the British Museum turned up an engraving of a contemporary portrait of Maria Malibran. The likeness between this picture from life, and Coral Polge's psychically received likeness is uncanny. It seems hardly likely that Coral Polge, producing more than 30 portraits a week, would have had time to research this one case in order to make an impression on Grace Brooks. And she certainly could not have been relying on telepathy to give her the image in Grace Brooks's mind.

THE STORY OF DOC TESTER

While Coral Polge gave up drawing portraits of spirit guides, there is a fascinating story concerning one portrait of a spirit guide that deserves to be retold. The picture involved so many different people in its long wait for its rightful home that it speaks for a real and mysterious consistency between psychics, and strongly suggests that there is a truth of some guides – and in the survival of the individual identity after death.

In medium Tom Fox's consulting room in his house in Copthorne, West Sussex, hangs the portrait in oils of a rough-and-ready character who might have ridden the frontier in the days of Wild Bill Hickok and Doc Holiday. The tale of how this picture came to be on Tom Fox's wall is told here in his own words, taken from his autobiography *Medium Rare*:

'In the late Sixties I went for a private reading with a very well-known and respected medium, Billy Elton, the founder of the Spiritualist church in Aylesbury, Buckinghamshire. Among other things he told me that one of my spirit guides was an Australian doctor, whose name, he said, was Dr Tester. Now I'd

Coral Polge with one of her portraits of a dead person, drawn through her awareness of their presence.

never heard, seen, or sensed such a person at all, let alone known that I had such a character as a spirit guide. But I made a note of the name in my diary, as I always do put down details of a reading, imagining as I did so that this was some kind of fresh-faced modern colonial type – white coat, blond hair, maybe with glasses, and a cheerful and cheering manner for his rounds of the hospital wards.

'About a year or two later (during which there was no sign of Dr Tester in any shape or form) I was doing trance work in a development circle run by my old and dear friend Hilda Kirby.

Among the members was another great friend, Jack Toyer. Just before we started one meeting – I remember he was sitting opposite me in the circle – Jack said, in a somewhat disapproving voice: "Tom… There's a spirit form, of a dirty old Mexican, standing behind you, you know."

"'Oh, is there?" I said. "Well, he's welcome. I don't know who he is, but he's welcome."

'I didn't give this "visitor" any more thought after that, because I soon went into trance. Blue Star, my Zulu guide, came through, and for some time was speaking through me about spiritual development and the world of Spirit. When he had finished Blue Star said, rather sternly, to Jack: "The man in the big black hat would like to talk to you."

'With that, he gave everyone a blessing and left, and I then started to come out of trance. I was nearly "round" when I suddenly went under again, under a very strong influence indeed. The person who'd taken control of me this time said - without any preamble, polite introductions, or anything: "Who the bloody hell d'ye think you're calling a dirty old Mexican? I'm no dirty old Mexican, mate. My name's Doc Tester."

'That caused a bit of stir in our polite gathering since nobody had any idea who that was, and I was in no position to tell them. Cutting right across the chatter, the blunt Doc just told them all to stop making so much noise and, in so many words, to shut up. Then he launched into quite a long talk about healing – and very lucid, very informative and, in fact, entertaining he was.

'Doc Tester is a very powerful character, but he's not intolerant: he gently and jovially mocks people, though, if he thinks they're not living up to the best in themselves. So that first appearance was also peppered with wisecracks at people who, he thought, were speaking without thinking, or asking him silly questions. And then, just as Blue Star had done, he offered everyone a blessing and, with a promise to return another time, departed.

'After the meeting, as usual, we had a cup of tea all round. I needed it: I kept thinking that that couldn't be the Dr Tester that Billy Elton had mentioned.

'I said to Jack: "Are you really sure he had black hair?"

'"Absolutely," he said. "And the black hat. He was a scruffy old thing."

'I still couldn't believe it. This wasn't exactly the clean-cut young man that, for some reason, I persisted in thinking "my" Dr Tester had to be. And, as it happened, I personally heard no more from, or about, Doc Tester for a long time – about four or five years, in fact.

'In the early Seventies, I went to the Spiritualist church at Aylesbury one Sunday – just as an ordinary member of the congregation – and sat down at the back. During the service I became aware of a couple sitting in front of me – for, standing between them, with his arms around them – cuddling them, in fact – was the very strong visible presence of a teenage boy. He was about fifteen, I'd say, slimly built, and quite tall.

'The lady of the couple was, it turned out, an officer of the church, and after the service she made a point of speaking to the new faces, like me, who'd come to the church for the first time that day. I told her about the boy I'd seen with his arms around her and her husband. She called her husband over at once, and had me repeat the description. "That's our son," they agreed. "He died experimenting with a plastic bag - pulled it over his head and died of asphyxiation. We know it wasn't suicide. Just a hideous accident."

'We had quite a conversation after that. Their names, I discovered, were Vic and Pam Bradford. The next thing I knew I was being invited to tea with them for the following weekend.

'When I arrived at their house, the first thing I saw on their living-room wall was an oil painting of a man dressed in black, with black hair, and a big black hat. At once I asked the lady of the house who he was.

"'You tell me," she said.

"'His name's Doc Tester, he's Australian, and he worked in the outback," I heard myself saying without thinking. "And that's all I know."

"'Then he's yours," she said. "He's been waiting here three years for you."I was completely amazed. How could anyone else know about Doc Tester – especially when even I had doubted that he actually looked like that? How had anyone been able to paint this picture, or be sure that I would get to know about it?

'Then Pam told me the story.

'For her and Vic it began a couple of years after Doc – unknown to them, of course – had surprised our development circle. In Northampton there was a medium called Jack Burrell. He was also a psychic artist, who specialized in pictures of the family, friends, and spirit guides of people who came to him for readings. There were two unusual things about his art. He would paint only people who were dead, whom he had never seen in the flesh or in photographs, and he always painted with his eyes closed, because he worked in a state of trance.

'Among the pictures of spirit guides he painted was a portrait in oils of a blackhaired man, who was wearing a black hat. Looking rather like a character from a Western, actually, except that in the background of the picture there are sheep, not long-horn steers.

'When Burrell had completed this picture, he gave it to his friends Pam and Vic Bradford.

"'It's not yours," he explained, "and it's not for you. But I want you to keep it. Hang it on your living-room wall. This is an Australian doctor, and he's somebody's healer in Spirit.

Someone will be along eventually to collect it. But that's all I can tell you."

'And there I was, looking at that painting, and knowing that this really was Doc Tester. The painting hangs on the wall of my consulting room now, a reminder and an inspiration to me always. I think Doc would be one of my favourite people, with his blunt speech, rambunctious style, and dry style of humour, and I treasure his picture.

'I've found out a bit more about him since – from himself and from others in Spirit. He was an ordinary, country doctor, working out in the Australian outback in the Twenties. He'd spend weeks at a time riding from station to station and settlement to settlement on horseback – which is why his clothes are always so scruffy: they're old, travelling clothes, and they're covered in dust from his journeys in the bush.

'To tell the truth, Doc has done more talking to people in development circles and the like than he has made himself felt by doing healing through me. On the few occasions that I have done healing I've known he's there, but he tends to stay in the background.'

PROOF AT LAST?

The authors of the Reader's Digest volume *Unsolved Mysteries of the Past* comment aptly on this singular example of psychic art: 'The most remarkable part of this story is that three mediums besides Fox himself independently either saw or were aware of Doc Tester, two of them before Fox had [learned] anything about his spirit guide; and the man who painted Tester's picture was someone whom Fox had never met.'

Whether or not they amount to proof of life after death, cases like this, and others – like Coral Polge's portrait of Maria Malibran – certainly confront us with a more than ordinary mystery.

VISIONS OF AN AFTERLIFE

After a routine operation, something went frighteningly wrong. The doctors brought Iris Lemov back to life within minutes – but she was no longer the same woman.

When Mrs Iris Lemov went into hospital for a routine operation neither she nor her doctors expected anything unusual to occur. What actually happened was to change her outlook on life – and death – altogether.

'I was brought back to my room after surgery,' she recalled in a journal article in November 1979, 'and was speaking to my nurse, when a strange separated feeling between my body and my brain occurred. High above my body I floated wondering why so many doctors were around my bed…'

Mrs Lemov had slipped suddenly and unexpectedly into a coma. But the abrupt dislocation of her consciousness and her body was not to be any ordinary out-of-the-body experience. For while she watched from above, she went deeper into coma and her heart stopped beating. To Mrs Lemov, looking down on the scene, it appeared only that her face had gone terribly pale. And then everything went suddenly dark.

She found herself sucked into a long black tunnel. Light glowed at the end of it. 'I felt frightened and excited as I neared the end of the tunnel,' she said. 'I felt peace, without pain, and free. The light at the end of the tunnel was bright but easy on my eyes.'

When she came out into the light, Iris Lemov found herself in a verdant, peaceful valley, which was 'a sight to behold. There was velvety green grass and calmness. Music coming from nowhere made me feel comfortable and I began to feel as if I belonged. I saw figures of people dressed in shrouds coming toward me and [they] called me by name. This man with a white beard told me to go back – your family still needs you – enjoy your life. This beautiful man was my grandfather who died two years before I was born…

'If we could all have the opportunity of seeing my valley during the course of our lifetime, how much more purposeful our lives would be.'

THROUGH THE MISTS

Iris Lemov's experience is typical of many who have clinically died, have been resuscitated and, in the brief period that they have been technically dead, have briefly visited the hereafter. Such people have, it seems, been vouchsafed a glimpse of the life after death. It is not surprising that the experience radically changes the attitude of most of these survivors toward death. For them, it no longer holds any fear, and, like Mrs Lemov's, their present lives are enriched as a result.

It is only with recent advances in medical technology – both drugs and equipment – that these 'near-death' experiences have been reported with any frequency – for the simple reason that they have allowed so many more people than ever before to be rescued from the very brink of death. But the truly striking thing about the reports of these brief sorties to the next world is their consistency. They may vary in detail, but the pattern of them is astonishingly uniform. Examples of other first-person accounts of such experiences will make this plain:

'I got up and walked into the hall to go get a drink, and it was at that point, as they found out later, that my appendix ruptured. I became very weak, and I fell down.

'I began to feel a sort of drifting, a movement of my real being in and out of my body, and to hear beautiful music. I floated on down the hall and out the door onto the screened-in porch. There, it almost seemed that clouds, a pink mist really, began to gather around me, and then I floated right straight on through the screen, just as though it weren't there, and up into this pure crystal clear light, an illuminating white light...

'It's not any kind of light you can describe on earth. I didn't actually see a person in this light, and yet it has a special identity ... It is a light of perfect understanding and perfect love.

'The thought came to my mind, "Thou lovest me?"' This was

not exactly in the form of a question, but I guess the connotation of what the light said was, "If you do love me, go back and complete what you began in your life." And all the time, I felt as though I were surrounded by an overwhelming love and compassion.'

A woman who collapsed from a heart attack reported:

'I found myself in a black void, and I knew I had left my physical body behind. I knew I was dying, and I thought, "God, I did the best I knew how at the time I did it. Please help me."

'Immediately, I was moved out of that blackness, through a pale grey, and I just went on, gliding and moving swiftly, and in front of me, in the distance, I could see a grey mist, and I was rushing toward it. It seemed that I just couldn't get to it fast enough… Beyond the mist, I could see people… and I could also

When near death, some people have reported seeing divine messengers as they slip out of contact with this life, as shown in the engraving above.

see something which one could take to be buildings. The whole thing was permeated with the most gorgeous light – a living, golden yellow glow… 'As I approached more closely, I felt certain I was going through that mist. It was such a wonderful, joyous feeling… Yet, it wasn't my time to go through the mist, because instantly from the other side appeared my uncle Carl, who had died many years earlier. 'He blocked my path, saying, "Go back. Your work on earth has not been completed. Go back now." I didn't want to go back, but I had no choice, and immediately I was back in my body. I felt that horrible pain in my chest, and I heard my little boy crying, "God, bring my mummy back to me."'

THERE AND BACK AGAIN

Those who have spent years collecting reports like these – the chief researchers include Drs Raymond Moody, Kenneth Ring, Margot Grey, Michael Rawlings and Michael Sabom – have compiled, from their analyses of hundreds of examples, a typical pattern of events that occur to people who are briefly clinically dead. They call this the 'core experience', on which almost every individual near-death experience is a variation.

This essential sequence of the journey from life to death and back is as follows:

as people begin to die, they feel a blissful sensation;

as clinical death occurs, they have an out-of-the-body experience, floating above the scene in which their body is lying;

they go into a misty, or more often a dark area, and most see this transformed into a long tunnel with light at the end;

they hurtle with increasing speed down the tunnel;

as they emerge into the light, they are greeted by a relative or by a recognised religious leader such as Jesus of Nazareth;

the scenery at the end of the tunnel is often pastoral – a pleasant rural scene, or a beautiful garden;

soothing or 'heavenly' music is playing, though often its source is invisible;

sometimes, scenes from their earthly life pass before them, as if in a movie. These may also occur earlier in the sequence, before or during the passage through the tunnel;

a disembodied voice from 'the light', or the relative or other figure who greeted them, tells them to 'go back';

the return from this celestial scene is usually instantaneous. At once, the body feels normal sensations – usually the pain from their injury or from the efforts of those trying to revive them;

as a result of the experience, people no longer fear death. They also tend to express a reduced interest in material things, and a heightened interest in spiritual matters, although conventional religions often lose much of any former attraction they may have had.

A PSYCHOLOGICAL TRICK?

The very consistency of the near-death experience argues for its truth: that there is a place we go when we die, and our loved ones are there to greet us and ease us past the shock of the transition from this life to the next. But that very same consistency can be interpreted in a quite different way.

For example, the highly regarded parapsychologist Dr Susan Blackmore has suggested that one near-death experience is so like another not because we all experience the same actual, objective reality at the point of death, but because our brains are essentially built in the same way – just as we all have noses above our mouths, and eyes to watch over both, and ears one each side of our heads. As our physical system collapses, the shards of consciousness interpret these symptoms of death in the best possible light, calling on the failing memory to create a marvellously benign and reassuring, but essentially fantastic, mental environment. Dr Blackmore concludes that 'what is generally now called the near-death experience is a psychological trick, played by the dying brain on the consciousness in order to lessen the trauma of dying. Essentially, this type of experience is the brain's last fling.'

Indeed it may be. But there are several aspects of near-death experiences as reported that don't fit with this analysis and that suggest there may be an objective reality to these accounts of what happens when we die. The very first problem with the sceptical view of near-death experiences is of its own making. What possible biological reason can there be for the mind (or brain) to have evolved a 'trick' to make dying easier to bear? How did the mind discover that it needed to learn this trick? How could anyone - other than through reincarnation, in which one suspects Dr Blackmore does not believe – inherit it?

Even if there is a materialist explanation for the near-death experience, this strange formula is hardly the best way to express it.

'GREETING FIGURES'

There are further facets of reported near-death experiences that indicate that something real lies behind them.

First, there is the figure who greets the migrating soul, or consciousness, on its arrival in the 'other' world. It would be interesting to know more about what distinguishes those who have been greeted on the 'other side' by standard religious figures such as Jesus, St Peter or the archangel Gabriel, from those who have been met only with a seemingly sentient, all-embracing, 'clear white light', and from those who have had close relations and loved ones there to meet them. While prior expectations may create what (or whom) one perceives at this point, the figure (or lack of it) that people see may depend on their earthly circumstances.

It would be peculiar indeed if someone who had had a lifetime of almighty conflicts with relatives were suddenly to be greeted with boundless love and cosmic wisdom by the very same wicked grandad who had beaten them as children. It would be equally startling if an agnostic, who had never been averse to the existence of a Great Creator but had long suspected the prophet of Nazareth to be a con man, were to find that the figure welcoming him to the paradisaical garden was none other than a smiling Jesus Christ himself - who would then add injury to insult by telling him to go back and finish his business on Earth.

Besides, there is a long and hardy tradition – within close-knit families, at least – of dead relatives coming to 'collect' a dying person and usher them into the next world. And from time to time these bailiffs of the grim reaper have been seen by people quite separate from the person who is dying.

D. Scott Rogo, in *The Return from Silence*, cites a fine instance of such an event from the memoirs of the New York nurse Margaret Moser:

'In the winter of 1948-9 I nursed a very sick old lady, Mrs Rosa B… She was residing at that time at the Savoy Plaza Hotel on Fifth Avenue, and up to the last she was mentally competent.

'Early one afternoon… Mrs B. had been asleep, but suddenly I saw her sit up and wave happily, her face all smiles. I turned my head toward the door, thinking one of her daughters had come in; but much to my surprise it was an elderly lady I had never seen before. She had a striking resemblance to my patient – the same light blue eyes, but a longer nose and a heavier chin. I could see her very clearly for it was bright daylight; the window shades were only slightly lowered. The

115

visitor walked toward my patient, bent down, and... they kissed each other. But then, as I got up and walked toward the bed, she was gone.

'Mrs B. looked very pleased. She took my hand and said, "It is my sister!" Then she slept peacefully again. I saw the same apparition twice later on, but never as clearly and always from another room. But every time she came the patient was obviously elated.'

Ms Moser later had corroborative evidence from her patient's sister's son that the apparition she and Mrs B. had both seen at the same time indeed resembled Mrs B.'s sister in all respects. Scott Rogo commented that 'this story... points to the objective existence of the "greeting figures" commonly seen by people having [near-death experiences]... We obviously need to collect more stories of this calibre...'

D. Scott Rogo, sadly, is himself now dead, but here is a small contribution to this needed literature, which was reported to the author of this book by a member of the family involved. (In the interest of privacy certain personal details have been changed.)

In 1979 an exiled Iranian princess lay terminally ill from cancer in her house in London, England. Her husband was a doctor with a busy practice, and care of the dying woman fell largely to her elder daughter, Imrana, who was then aged about 14. She was with her mother in her final hours. At some point during that time, when it was obvious that no recovery was possible, the dying princess announced that her own father and an uncle, both long since dead, had arrived in her room.

She actually went so far as to introduce her daughter to the pair, although to Imrana they remained steadfastly invisible. Despite her feebleness, the fading woman then told them to go away, since she wasn't 'ready for them' yet. Apparently they did, for she soon ceased to be troubled by their presence. She next

116

gave her daughter a long lecture on her future duties to the family. This responsibility discharged, she settled herself to wait for her 'guides' to come back to collect her. Her daughter saw her greet them before she finally gave up the ghost.

SWEET MELODIES

There is, then, some evidence that the 'greeting figures' reported by those who have had near-death experiences do have some objective existence. There is also evidence that the celestial music that dying people hear from, or in, the next world is not entirely of their own desperate imagining.

In a more peaceful representation in a French 12th-century manuscript, Christ is shown as supreme judge.

A close friend of a certain Mrs L. recorded the simultaneous experiences of several friends of the lady who, with her son, had gathered at her bedside shortly before she died in 1881. The report was given to Edmund Gurney, a senior member of the Society for Psychical Research in London, on 28 July that year, and it stated:

'Just after dear Mrs L.'s death between 2 and 3 a.m., I heard a most sweet and singular strain of singing outside the windows; it died away after passing the house. All [but one] in the room heard it, and the medical attendant, who was still with us, went to the window, as I did, and looked out, but there was nobody [outside]. It was a bright and beautiful night.

'It was as if several voices were singing in perfect unison a most sweet melody which died away in the distance. Two persons had gone from the room to fetch something and were coming upstairs at the back of the house and heard the singing... They could not, naturally, have heard any sound from outside the windows in the front of the house from where they were in the back.'

The only person who did not hear this sweet music was Mrs L.'s son, although the family doctor (the 'medical attendant') independently corroborated all the details of the first report, adding that the music consisted of 'a few bars... not unlike that from an aeolian harp – and it filled the air for a few seconds'. In his book quoted earlier, D. Scott Rogo remarked: 'The fact that the patient's son didn't hear the music implies that the sounds weren't from the street, but represented some form of psychic process.' He himself collected a number of reports of similar codas to people's lives, although they seemed to be rare in 20th-century experience.

Finally, the view that the near-death experience is imaginary, a 'trick' dictated by biology and designed to obscure the fact of death, falls down over a crucial phase in the core experience.

In fact the sceptics do not even address this question. And that is: if the experience is essentially imaginary, how does the imagination manage to put the procedure so neatly into reverse, as it were, when resuscitation is successful, and produce a suitable figure to pronounce the words 'Go back – your business on Earth is not yet finished' (or phrases to that effect), time after time, in so many different people? This is a surprising and unexpected sub-routine to find in a biological programme supposedly designed to ease one into oblivion.

The light above the clouds. Some people who have had near-death experiences have felt they have risen above earthly things.

THE FINAL CURTAIN

It might be argued that near-death experiences must be imaginary because they are simply too good to be true: no doubt most people would like to find themselves in green pastures and pleasant company on the other side of death. But not everyone who has glimpsed beyond that final curtain has had such a comforting vision. Some have seen Hell.

'I found myself in a place surrounded by mist... There was a big pit with vapour coming out and there were arms and hands coming out trying to grab mine... I was terrified that these hands were going to claw hold of me and pull me into the pit,' one such unfortunate told researcher Dr Margot Grey.

Another told Dr Raymond Moody that, as he travelled toward the realm of light during his near-death experience, he passed a place of terrible desolation, full of 'washed out', only partly human forms with an 'absolute, crushed, hopeless demeanour', who 'seemed to be forever shuffling, moving around, not knowing where they were going, not knowing who to follow, or what to look for'.

Both these kinds of Hell have been reported by more than one witness. As Dr Michael Rawlings puts it, with black humour: 'It may not be safe to die.' Furthermore, the existence of the place of dreadful desolation has had some degree of objective verification.

APPALLING SORROW

In 1961, when serving with the British Army in Germany, medium Tom Fox spent a night at the site of the former Nazi concentration camp, Bergen-Belsen. He dozed off, and then:

'I woke up, and something very like Hell itself flooded my mind.

'No more than five yards away, clearly visible, there was a man standing. He was pale and thin, and a sense of appalling sorrow was welling from him.

'It very soon became obvious that he was by no means alone. His was the only form I could see, but I rapidly became aware of the presence of a whole crowd of souls. Occasionally, at the edge of things, I would see their blurred or fleeting images, as if they were on the brink of becoming visible… But there was no doubting that they were there. For I could hear them clearly enough. I was being overwhelmed with the turmoil of their suffering and heartbreak. At first I tried to close myself off from the agonised clamour of those tormented spirits. They were speaking in their own languages, incomprehensible to me, but their anguish was unmistakable… Then, as I calmed down, I was able to distinguish personal voices and individual emotions.

'Some were consumed with the desire for vengeance; others asked only to be released from the nightmare of their experience, or to be freed from Belsen itself, the place to which they had become bound by their suffering. So many people had endured so many dreadful things in that camp, and in so short a time, that to those who had been there, it seemed that only those souls who had shared that terrible experience could possibly comprehend its enormity. Their time in Belsen had become their only reality. And so they had remained, tied to the place, to comfort one another.'

Fox prayed for them, and eventually the tormented host faded away. But, said Fox 'I have had learned more about human pain in those few hours at Belsen than many people do in a lifetime.' The near-death experience seems to offer the best evidence so far that there is a life beyond death – and that, as might be expected, it is as challenging in its own way as life on Earth.

ABRAHAM LINCOLN

The ghostly shape of Abraham Lincoln, America's 16th and most acclaimed president, is said to still walk the corridors of power inside the White House to this very day! The assassinated Lincoln is a particularly distinguished ghost.

While the settings for many hauntings often involve gloomy buildings, fog-shrouded nights and isolated surroundings, there are some ghosts that would seem to prefer a more crowded, more open environment.

Indeed, everyone from Winston Churchill to presidents and visiting heads of state have claimed to have seen the ghost of 'Honest Abe' at 1600 Pennsylvania Avenue. Former President Ronald Reagan's eldest daughter, Maureen, recalled just a few years ago that she, too, had seen it. 'I'm not kidding,' says Maureen. 'We've really seen it.' She and her husband, Dennis Revell, often slept in Lincoln's bedroom when they visited her parents in Washington, and claim to have seen the apparition, which sometimes glows a bright red, sometimes orange. Maureen and her husband claim that it is Lincoln's ghost. 'When I told my parents what I saw, they looked at me a little weirdly,' she admitted.

Eleanor Roosevelt, the wife of President Roosevelt, often thought she could feel Lincoln's presence when she was up late at night, writing in her diary. And President Harry Truman, who served from 1945 to 1952, also claimed to have heard Lincoln's ghost walking through the building.

The most detailed sighting, however, came from Dutch Queen Wilhelmina, who stayed as a guest at the Roosevelt White House. One night, after hearing footsteps outside her bedroom, she opened the door and, to her amazement, there stood Lincoln, complete with his trademark top hat. Queen Wilhelmina was so overcome by the sight, that she fainted to the floor with a heavy thud! With the exception of Maureen Reagan, there have been few sightings in recent years, though Nancy Reagan recalled that Rex, the family dog, would often sit outside the haunted bedroom and bark at the door for no apparent reason – and the pooch steadfastly refused ever to set paw in it.

In real life, Abraham Lincoln was a dedicated follower of the paranormal for much of his adult life, attending numerous seances, and several times he had chilling premonitions and nightmares of his own assassination. His wife, Mary Todd, whom he married in 1842, was also a firm believer in seances, and that same year Lincoln wrote to a friend explaining that 'I have always had a strong tendency to mysticism', and often felt that he was controlled 'by some other power than my own will'. However, it wasn't until the death of his favourite son, Willie, several years later, that he became a devotee of seances. He tried on many occasions to contact his dear departed son, but he never succeeded.

An artist's impression of President Abraham Lincoln's murder.

When he became President in 1860, he was often a guest at seances, and one medium, Cora Maynard, a friend of his wife, even claimed that she was responsible for Lincoln's landmark emancipation proclamation of 1 January 1863, which ordered the release of every slave in the United States! Mrs Maynard maintained that Lincoln issued the order after spirits told him to do so. While American historians doubt that a man of Lincoln's convictions would have issued so important an order simply to placate the spirit world, some agree that it might have bolstered his long-held belief that slavery was morally wrong.

It was a belief that would eventually cost him his life. On 14 April 1865, just three months into his second term of office and just five days after the southern Confederate forces surrendered to end the bloody Civil War, Lincoln attended the opening of a new play, *My American Cousin*, at the Ford Theater in Washington, DC, with his wife and several dignitaries. Shortly after the curtain went up, a disgruntled Southerner, John Wilkes Booth, calmly walked into the presidential box and shot Lincoln in the head. He died the next morning.

Yet, incredibly, Lincoln had had numerous 'forewarnings' of his own death, and on the very day he was shot, he had remarked to his chief bodyguard that he had been having nightmares about his murder. His first premonition, however, came just prior to his election in 1860, when he saw a strange image of himself in a mirror. Next to his reflection was another image of himself, deathly pale in colour. When he tried to stare at it, it vanished. This was to happen several times during the course of his time in the White House, and wife Mary concluded that it meant he would serve two terms, but not survive the second!

Then, in the days leading up to his ill-fated trip to the Ford theater - which he had only attended because Mary had wanted to – he had a series of macabre, disturbing dreams. In his diary, he wrote about one of these vivid nightmares:

Visitors to the White House, including Winston Churchill, have claimed to have seen Lincoln's ghost.

A DREAM OF DEATH

'I retired late. I soon began to dream. There seemed to be a death-like stillness about me. Then I heard subdued sobs, as if a number of people were weeping. I thought I had left my bed and wandered downstairs. There the silence was broken by the same pitiful sobbing, but the mourners were invisible. I went from room to room; no living person was in sight, but the same mournful sounds of distress met me as I passed. It was light in all the rooms; every object was familiar to me; but where were all the people who were grieving as if their hearts would break?

'I was puzzled and alarmed. What could be the meaning of all this? Determined to find the cause of a state of things so mysterious and so shocking, I kept on until I arrived at the East Room, which I entered. Before me was a catafalque, on which rested a corpse wrapped in funeral vestments. Around it were stationed soldiers who were acting as guards; and there was a throng of people, some gazing mournfully upon the corpse, whose face was covered, others weeping pitifully.

'"Who is dead in the White House?" ' I demanded of one of the soldiers. "The President," was his answer. "He was killed by an assassin." Then came a loud burst of grief from the crowd, which awoke me from my dream. I slept no more that night; and although it was only a dream, I have been strangely annoyed by it ever since.'

On the very day prior to his death, Lincoln even confided to one of his Cabinet members that he had had premonitions of the murder, and told his head bodyguard, W.H. Cook, that he had dreamed of his assassination for three straight nights. The startled guard begged the much loved President not to attend the opening, but Lincoln simply sighed and said he had promised Mary they would go. He never came out alive.

Following the state funeral service in Washington, Lincoln's body was transported by train to his home state of Illinois. But more than 100 years later, there are still some people who claim to have seen a phantom train, draped in black bunting, slowly wending its way along the same route to Illinois. Many years ago, an account of this sad phenomenon was recorded in an article carried in the *Evening Times*, a newspaper in Albany, New York:

'Regularly in the month of April, about midnight, the air on the tracks becomes very keen and cutting. On either side of the tracks, it is warm and still. Every watchman, when he feels the air, slips off the track and sits down to watch. Soon the pilot engine of Lincoln's funeral train passes along with long, black streamers and with a band of black instruments playing dirges, grinning skeletons all about.

'It passes noiselessly. If it is moonlight, clouds come over the moon as the phantom train goes by. After the pilot engine passes, the funeral train itself with flags and streamers rushes past. The track seems covered with black carpet, and the coffin is seen in the centre of the car, while all about it in the air and on the train behind are vast numbers of blue-coated men, some with coffins on their backs, others leaning upon them.'

STRANGE OCCURRENCES

'If a real train were passing, its noise would be hushed as if the phantom train rode over it. Clocks and watches always stop as the phantom train goes by and when looked at are five to eight minutes behind. Everywhere on the road about 27 April watches and clocks are suddenly found to be behind.'

It is also interesting to note that some months after the President was assassinated by Booth, his wife posed for a photographer – when the plate was developed, there was a foggy resemblance of Lincoln standing right there next to Mary.

For almost 60 years after Lincoln died, there were no known reports of his ghost inside the White House. But when Calvin Coolidge became the 29th President in 1923, following the death of Warren Harding, the ghost made its first known appearance. Coolidge's wife, Grace, recalled seeing Lincoln's shadow standing at the window inside the Oval Office, which is the presidential seat of power. It was only visible for a few seconds, and seemed to be looking forlornly towards the Potomac river, which wends its way into the distance. Incredibly, during Lincoln's term of office, he had once stood at that very same window, and was described by Army chaplain E.C. Bolles as looking thoroughly despondent. 'I think I never saw so sad a face in my life, and I have looked into many a mourner's face,' Bolles later recorded in his journal.

Following Grace Coolidge's experience, many other powerful and important people also claimed to have seen or heard the spectre of President Lincoln. But there have been no reported incidents since Maureen Reagan's encounter in the late 1980s. That is not to say, however, that Lincoln has finally given up the ghost on the White House! Maybe we will have to wait until George and Laura Bush leave office to know if they, too, heard or saw anything of Honest Abe.

HAMPTON COURT

Like President Lincoln, some other ghosts also prefer a more crowded environment than the traditional haunt. Such is the case with the spirits of Hampton Court, in Middlesex, which has been home to a series of unexplained events for centuries. Various ghosts have been sighted within its surrounds, including the puzzling case of the fair-haired boy. Before World War Two, the Old Court House, which was home to Sir Christopher Wren while he supervised renovations to the palace, was owned by a man called Norman Lamplugh. On a lovely summer's day, as guests mingled on the lawn, Norman's brother Ernest and another man, who were looking out across the gardens from a staircase, suddenly spotted a young boy aged about eight walking across the lawn. They looked at each other quizzically, for not only had Norman not invited any children to the garden party, but the fair-haired lad was clad in a page boy suit from the time of King Charles II, who died in 1685! His costume was authentic right down to the big silver buckles on his shoes!

The mysterious youngster then entered the house, and walked up the stairs right past the two startled guests. He said nothing, and seemed to not even notice them. He then walked down the hall, entering a room which had only one entrance, the one leading off the hall. The two men quickly followed the young guest into the room, but could find no trace of him!

The palace has been home to ghosts for more than 400 years.

But there are said to be ghosts at Hampton Court which pre-date even a 17th-century page boy. During the reign of Henry VIII, the king's third wife, Jane Seymour, gave birth to a son, in October 1537, at Hampton Court. Tragically, the baby died just seven days later. For hundreds of years ever since, people have reported seeing Queen Jane's ghost, clad all in white, gliding through the Court, her way lit by a taper, on the anniversary of the child's death. Many have seen her presence come from a doorway in the Queen's Old Apartments, then wander silently down the stairway where she disappears into a gallery. Two servants who saw the apparition described her as 'a tall lady, with a long train and shining face'.

Then there was the case of the two Cavaliers who haunted Fountain Court. They were seen earlier last century by Lady Hildyard, who complained about their appearance and the strange noises she heard from her apartment which overlooked the Court. A short time later, a work crew was sent down to install new drains in the Court, and workers discovered the remains of two Cavaliers, buried just a few feet below the pavement. They were disinterred and given a proper burial, and that was the last anyone ever heard from them.

Not so the so-called White Lady of Hampton Court who was spotted by fishermen as recently as the 1960s. There are also said to be ghosts of the headless Archbishop Laud, who has been spotted walking quietly inside the hallowed halls of the Court, and Mrs Sybil Penn, who was the nurse of Edward VI. Mrs Penn, a kindly soul who tended like a mother to the sickly young prince, and retired to an apartment inside Hampton Court after her service was done. She caught smallpox, and died in November 1568. She was buried at St Mary's Church, close to the Court, and remained there at rest for more than 250 years, until the church was struck by lightning and destroyed in 1829. Her tomb was taken to the site of the new church, but tragically her grave was vandalized and her remains scattered.

A short while later, her ghost was seen back at the apartment she had once lived in. At that time, a family was living there and they often heard the sound of a woman's voice and a spinning wheel. After making complaints, a team of workmen were brought in to check out the noises. They found a secret chamber leading off one of the rooms in the apartment – and inside, they found a spinning wheel, which was thought to be the one used by Mrs Penn some 300 years earlier! After the chamber was discovered, the ghost of Mrs Penn was itself seen for the first time. A guard on duty outside her apartment looked up one day to see a woman, dressed in a long robe and hood, coming from inside the rooms. The ghostly figure then vanished. He later claimed that the woman bore a striking resemblance to the stone replica of Mrs Penn. Princess Frederica of Hanover, who had heard nothing about the ghost, also claimed to have seen Mrs Penn, this time in a long grey robe with a hood over her head. Since then, her ghost has been known as the Lady in Grey.

In the years since, many others have had brushes with the royal nurse. Servants have been woken in the dead of night by an icy hand touching their heads; they've heard footsteps and crashing sounds with no earthly explanation. Once, servants claimed they entered the vacant apartment and found it awash in 'a ghastly, lurid light'. But of all the ghosts said to inhabit Hampton Court, none has achieved the notoriety of the one believed to be the spirit of Lady Katherine Howard, Henry VIII's fifth wife, who was 19 when the King was first captivated by her charms. Lady Katherine was a tiny, waif-like girl, but no stranger to romance. She had had numerous suitors before she married Henry in July 1540, and continued her affairs even after she became his wife and Queen. Indeed, her love life was so hectic that enemies later chided her for living 'an abominable, base, carnal, voluptuous and vicious life', and branded her 'a harlot'.

She was eventually arrested on 12 November 1541, for her wayward lifestyle, but on the very night before she was taken away to the dreaded Tower of London for eventual execution by beheading, she begged Henry to spare her life. Her pleas fell on deaf ears, and Henry even watched in stony silence as she was dragged away by his sentries to meet her horrible fate. Over the centuries, her ghost is said to appear every 11 November running and screaming through what is today known

*King Henry VIII . . . several of his wives and servants
are said to still call Hampton Court home!*

as the Haunted Gallery. Numerous people have seen the ghastly apparition, and all describe it as a woman with long, flowing locks.

In the mid-1800s, the Haunted Gallery was closed and its space used for storing pictures. But a lady living in an apartment next door claimed that one night she was awoken from a sound sleep by a hideous scream which seemed to be coming from inside the Gallery. A short time later, a friend staying with her also heard the blood-curdling shriek.

But probably the most eerie story concerning Queen Katherine came after the Haunted Gallery was eventually reopened. An artist, who was doing a sketch of an old tapestry hanging on the wall, was stunned to see a disembodied hand appear right in front of it. The quick-thinking artist drew the free-floating hand, and the ring that it wore. Incredibly, the ring was later identified as one often worn by Katherine.

Yet another of Henry's wives, Anne Boleyn, is said to haunt Hampton Court. She was spotted about 100 years ago by a servant, who recognized her from her portrait. She was dressed completely in blue, and vanished within seconds. Her ghost has been spotted at several other sites around England, including the Tower, Hever Castle, Rochford Hall and Salle Church.

There have been other reports of hauntings at Hampton Court, though none of the ghosts could be identified. During World War Two, a policeman on duty saw 11 people on the palace grounds simply vanish into thin air, while stage actor Leslie Finch, who had just completed a play at the site, saw a Tudor-clad figure that vanished, leaving behind only a sudden iciness in the air. Similarly in 1966, a member of the audience viewing a light and sound display saw the ghost of Cardinal Thomas Wolsey, who gave the palace to Henry VIII, standing under one of the archways.

The Palace of Versailles – site of several paranormal events.

VERSAILLES

Although not as overrun by ghosts as Hampton Court, the great Palace of Versailles, just outside Paris, has some of the most intriguing tales of haunting ever recorded. In fact, this monument to the grandeur of pre-Revolutionary France was the site of a major investigation into psychic phenomena. Since 1870, there had been reports of 100-year-old apparitions not only of people, but also of buildings (!) within the Petit Trianon at Versailles, but it wasn't until 1902 that a painstaking analysis of the sightings was finally undertaken.

In 1762, Louis XV ordered the Petit Trianon built for his mistress, the beautiful Marquise de Pompadour, but she never lived to see its completion. However, when the house was finally finished in 1770, the King had by then taken another mistress, Madame Dubarry, who lived inside the estate occasionally. A carriageway led from the house to the King's farm at Versailles, called the Allée de la Managerie. Over the next few years, further work was carried out on the site. In 1773 a chapel was added, but its construction meant the carriageway had to be closed, and some of it was destroyed. Following Louis's death in 1774, the Petit Trianon was given to Marie Antoinette by the new king, Louis XVI, and she used it until the bloody Revolution ended the royal reign of the Bourbons (for the next 25 years).

Our story really begins on 10 August, 1901, when Eleanor Jourdain and Annie Moberly, both British scholars and the daughters of respected clergymen, were visiting the Palace of Versailles during a holiday stay in France. Although both were well educated, neither had any particular knowledge of the royal compound which could account for the stunning developments to come.

After wandering through the Grand Trianon where the Age of Kings has been resplendently captured in time, the two friends began walking towards the Petit Trianon. Given the vast size of Versailles, it is not surprising to learn that the two women soon found that they had become completely lost. However, they eventually came to the garden, which they entered. Moberly would later recall that when they did so, she felt 'an extraordinary depression'. Jourdain, too, was somehow aware of a strange feeling inside the garden, and both ladies felt a little ill at ease.

STRANGE FIGURES

Oddly, they later recounted, there had been a strong breeze blowing that day, and yet when they arrived at the Petit Trianon, the air had turned deathly still. Not a leaf moved. As they walked onwards, they suddenly noticed two strange-looking men. The women believed them to be gardeners, although they thought it a little odd that both men were dressed in 18th-century costumes, with greenish coats and tricorn hats. Later, Moberly recalled that 'I began to feel as if I were walking in my sleep; the heavy dreaminess was oppressive.'

Undaunted, the British holidaymakers asked the men for directions, and were told to continue their trek straight ahead. As they did, they saw a bridge and a kiosk. Sitting near the kiosk, they observed a curious-looking man in a slouch-hat and coat. Both women felt a little put off by his appearance. Suddenly, they heard footsteps behind them. They turned and a man with 'a curious smile' and strange accent gave them more directions. They believed him to be one of the gardeners they had just met. He vanished as suddenly as he had appeared.

As they neared the house, Moberly saw yet another figure, this time a woman, who was sitting on a small seat on the grass. She, too, was dressed in authentic period costume. A few seconds later, they watched as a young man, also smiling strangely, walked from the house using a solid door – a door they would later discover had been broken and left in ruins for many years. They also noticed the carriageway, which had been obliterated more than 130 years earlier!

The bizarre experience lasted for some 30 minutes, and afterwards both women concurred that the Petit Trianon had to be haunted. For the next ten years, these two well-educated ladies returned several times to the site in the hope that they could finally solve the mystery that had so disturbed them. Jourdain made a second visit a year later, and once more she felt the same oppressive atmosphere that seemed to hover over the area. As she crossed the small bridge that led to the former house of Marie Antoinette, she came across two workmen who wore the costumes of 18th century French labourers, right up to their pointed hoods. She also remembered hearing the sound of distant music. However she was no closer to solving the mystery.

Moberly joined her for yet another visit, this time on 4 July 1904. Oddly, they could no longer find the paths they had taken earlier, and there was no sign of the kiosk or the bridge! Both had literally vanished into thin air. Moreover, the spot where they had seen the woman sitting was now occupied by an old bush, which had been obviously growing there for many, many years.

A CAPTIVATING RIDDLE

The two women were by now completely enthralled by the riddle of the Petit Trianon, and for the next six years, they researched its entire history, firmly believing they had somehow 'seen' the site as it had appeared in the late 1700s. Upon completing their research, they wrote a book, *An Adventure*, in which they came to deduce that the woman they had seen sitting on the grass had in fact been Marie Antoinette herself! They came to this conclusion when they discovered that that particular spot had been a favourite of hers.

They also identified the two gardeners as the Bersey brothers, who had been employed to work on the estate by the Queen. Despite their years of research, however, the women were treated with scorn and derision upon the release of their book. However, the book was a popular success, and it prompted other holiday-makers to come forward with similar bizarre tales of Versailles.

One such visitor was Englishman John Crooke who had taken his wife and young son to Versailles in the summer of 1908. However, their ghostly encounter came in the Grand

Trianon, where they saw a woman sketching on some paper. She wore a long, cream skirt and a white hat. Crooke recalled that she paid no attention to them until he tried to get a peek at what she was drawing so intently. She grabbed her sketch so he couldn't see it, and then shot him an angry look. Suddenly, she disappeared. A short time later, the Crooke family saw two more strangely dressed people, who similarly vanished into thin air.

There were many other sightings to come over the years, some as recently as 1955. In 1928, two women, Clare Burrow and Ann Lambert, both English, went on a trip to Versailles. Neither had read the book written by Moberly and Jourdain, and yet they reportedly had a similar adventure. As they walked towards the Petit Trianon, Burrow, like Moberly 27 years earlier, suddenly felt an eerie languor. As they got closer, they saw an elderly, sinister-looking man, dressed in an 18th-century uniform. Despite his appearance, they asked him for directions, but ran off when he began shouting at them in guttural French. When they looked back at him, he had vanished. Throughout the course of the afternoon, they saw several other people all dressed in period clothes.

Ten years later, Elizabeth Hatton was strolling alone through the same grounds when from out of nowhere a man and woman, dressed like peasants, walked past her, pulling a wooden cart. When she turned to watch them, they slowly vanished before her very eyes. Many others have had similar experiences with vanishing people. In October 1949, Jack Wilkinson, his wife Clara, and their young son were touring the Grand Trianon. They noticed a woman, in 18th-century attire, holding an umbrella on the steps of the Grand Trianon. A few seconds later, she was gone.

One of the last recorded sightings came in May 1955, when a British lawyer and his wife walked towards the Petit Trianon. Like others before her, the woman felt a sudden depression, and then she and her husband spotted two men and a woman. Each was clad in the clothing suitable for French aristocracy before the Revolution. The men wore knee-length coats, black breeches, black shoes with silver buckles and black hats. The woman looked dazzling in a long yellow dress. Like other apparitions seen over the decades, they vanished into thin air without a trace to mark their appearance.

Sightings like these prompted much speculation about the existence of ghosts and other phenomena at Versailles. Many were sceptical, espousing the belief that all the startled visitors had simply seen people clad in the often-unfamiliar costumes of their native lands! Later, French writer Philippe Jullian would also claim that there was nothing sinister at all about the sightings. He said the poet Robert de Montesquiou and his friends would often dress up in period costume when they visited the Petit Trianon around the turn of the century. Yet Jullian's theory does not explain why there were sightings well into the second half of the 20th century, or how Montesquiou and his party could simply vanish without a trace.

Famed psychic researcher G.W. Lambert, who later wrote a book on the Versailles hauntings, believed in their validity. Using historical data available on Versailles, he concluded that the two gardeners first seen by Moberly and Jourdain were not brothers, but a father and son, Claude Richard and Antoine. However, he felt that the two English women had somehow seen Versailles as it would have appeared in 1770, and therefore the woman they saw sitting on the grass could not have been Marie Antoinette. Of course, the actual date is of little significance. After all, seeing something literally from out of the past is still incredibly bizarre, whether it dates back to 1770 or post-1774 when Marie Antoinette first came to the Petit Trianon.

In the final analysis, the hauntings of Versailles must be considered a puzzling mystery to this day.

Marie Antoinette, whose ghost was spotted at Versailles.

HAUNTED HOUSES

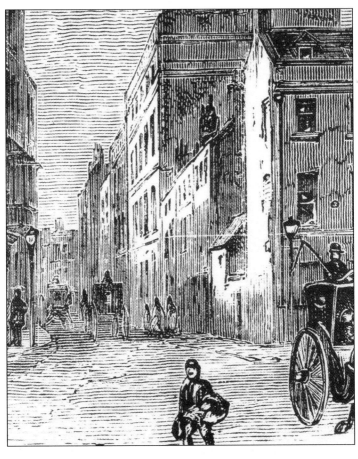

Few ghost stories are more terrifying or bone-chilling than those of spooky addresses… because a ghost in the house can strike anyone at anytime. Even now, some of the most notorious haunted houses in history remain legendary.

Today, the site at 50 Berkeley Square is not unlike other buildings in that fashionable area of inner London. Now a bookstore, with its stately elegance intact, it was once a grand old home, and even the residence of short-term Prime Minister George Canning, who owned it until his death in 1827. But 100 years ago, young children would cross the street to avoid it. Women, and even men, would walk quickly past it, lest some unseen force somehow reach out onto the street and grab them. All over the capital, people feared and loathed the site as a place of evil and malevolence.

Fifty Berkeley Square, you see, was said to be haunted! And not just by some ghostly apparition that occasionally moaned or rattled the pots and pans, but by a real evil – a murderous malevolence so ghastly that as many as four people were said to have been literally scared to death by the very sight of it, while others were driven to total insanity, unable to ever fully explain what had so terrified them.

The story of 50 Berkeley Square begins in 1859, when a Mr Myers took over the house. According to reports at the time, the poor man was left standing at the altar by his one true love and from that day on he shunned society and turned into a bitter, cynical recluse, rarely seen in public or even outside the house. The story goes that he moved all his belongings into a cramped, tiny room in the garret, and would see no one except his manservant who brought him his daily meals. At night, however, while the rest of London slept or partied into the late hours, Mr Myers would mournfully walk the cobwebbed corridors of the house, his way lit by a single candle. Over the years, as he became even more eccentric, the once-proud house fell into disrepair, its windows caked with thick black dust and grime.

In 1873, when Mr Myers failed to pay his local taxes, he was summoned to appear before the city council. But the weird loner steadfastly refused to even answer it. Despite his refusal, however, local officials decided not to take the matter any further – because they had heard the house was haunted and felt sympathy for the wretched man so unhinged by his unrequited love. Matters grew steadily worse for Mr Myers and within six years the house had become so notorious that London newspapers began writing articles on it and its strange legend. After Myers' death, terrified neighbours claimed they could still hear loud thumps, moans and sobbing coming from inside, and some reports claimed that even pieces of furniture would inexplicably move around the house.

One of the many tales surrounding the origins of the 50 Berkeley Square haunting tells of a young child who was either tortured or frightened to death in the house's nursery. The tot's forlorn ghost, still sobbing and wearing a plaid skirt, is said to make periodic appearances. Another story claims that the ghost is actually that of a young woman, who shared the house with her lascivious, miscreant uncle. In a final, desperate attempt to

One of the most evil ghosts ever recorded in the annals of the paranormal lay in wait at number 50 Berkeley Square.

at last free herself of his immoral advances, the young woman is said to have thrown herself from a window on the top floor to her death. For some time afterwards, people in the neighbourhood claimed to have seen her ghost, hanging on to the ledge, screaming for help. Eventually, there were so many sightings of various phenomena that the house actually became a tourist spot, so widespread was its infamy!

A CLUB OF SCEPTICS

But not everyone was ready to concede that it was haunted by unseen forces, and many believed that the cause of all the commotion could definitely be explained. Sir Robert Warboys was one such sceptic and, on a challenge from some fellow members of his club, he reportedly offered to spend a night inside the vacant house to prove that the bizarre tales of ghosts and evil were complete rubbish.

But the owner at this time, a Mr Benson, was reluctant to allow the bet to go ahead unless Sir Robert promised to take some precautions, including arming himself. Warboys good-naturedly agreed, and also took with him a bell Mr Benson had given him, which he could ring if anything went awry. Still, Sir Robert thought it all one big joke, and as he bade his friends good night, he scoffed at Benson nevertheless: 'My dear fellow,' he said, 'I am here to disprove the bunkum of a ghost, so your little alarm will be of no use. I bid you good night.'

With that, Sir Robert went upstairs. It was the last time anyone ever saw him alive. According to the story, all was well for the next 45 minutes. But suddenly, the little bell began to ring furiously from inside the bedroom. Then a shot was heard. People dashed up the creaky stairs, thrust open the bedroom door and found the limp body of Sir Robert sprawled across the bed. He had not been shot, but rather he is believed to have been literally frightened to death. His death mask was a face of sheer horror. His eyes bulged, and his mouth was frozen in twisted terror. His death only fuelled speculation that an intense evil lurked inside the house.

GUARANTEED PROTECTION

Not surprisingly then, the old house remained closed for some time afterwards until, in 1878, another well-heeled citizen, Lord Lyttleton, decided to follow in Sir Robert's footsteps by also daring to spend a night inside the haunted house. He, too, vowed to get to the bottom of the mystery and won permission from the new owner to spend a night in the very bedroom where Warboys had died some time before. But as a precaution, he took along with him two rifles which he had loaded with buckshot and silver sixpences, which folklore dictated would guarantee protection against whatever evil dwelt inside the room. During the course of that long, lonely night, Lyttleton got very little sleep as he tossed and turned, but once he did drift off he was suddenly awoken by a mysterious, grotesque shape that lunged at him from out of the dark. He managed to get off one shot at the apparition, which then vanished right before his startled eyes. Lyttleton was clearly shaken by his macabre experience, and wrote about his encounter in a book, *Notes and Queries*, which was published the following year.

SUPERNATURALLY FATAL

In it, the former sceptic conceded that 50 Berkeley Square was 'supernaturally fatal to mind and body'. For years afterwards, the aristocrat devoted much of his spare time to researching the macabre history of the house, and eventually located a woman who he said was driven insane after spending just one night inside the place. However, like so many others, Lyttleton could not determine why the ghost was so evil or what caused it to appear in such a hideous manner.

Another victim of that house of horrors was a new maid, whose terrifying ordeal was reported in *Mayfair* magazine. One night, after the household had long ago retired to bed, the owners were startled from their sleep by the maid's terrifying screams. They scrambled upstairs and entered her room, where they found her standing in the middle of her bedroom, 'rigid as a corpse, with hideously glaring eyes'. The poor girl was so overcome with terror, that she could not even utter a single word. She was taken to St George's Hospital, where doctors examined her and then asked her what had scared her so horribly. But the poor creature was too overcome to reply, and steadfastly refused to discuss the events of the previous night, saying only it was 'just too horrible' to describe. Her doctors never did get her to talk – because she died the very next day!

Yet another horrifying story of Berkeley Square concerns the macabre tale of two sailors, Edward Blunden and Robert Martin, who came to London on shore leave from the frigate HMS *Penelope.* It was Christmas Eve, and they had much trouble finding a room for the night. Freezing from the cold they eventually came upon 50 Berkeley Square, which was vacant at the time, so the seamen forced open a window and decided to sleep there. They came across a bedroom, which had been at the centre of all the previous sightings, and unwittingly bedded down for the night.

Blunden, however, had trouble falling asleep. He was nervous that someone might discover that they had broken into the house and summon the police to arrest them. He thought his fears had come true when he soon heard footsteps coming up the stairs. He was beside himself with panic, fearing that a policeman must have discovered the forced window and that he would be spending the night in a cold, damp jail cell.

He quickly woke Martin, and both heard the footsteps moving ever closer to the bedroom door. Then, the door opened, and both saw a hideous spectre coming towards them. Blunden quickly leaped to his feet, and made a grab for a heavy object resting on the nearby mantelpiece. He wasn't quick enough, however, and the ghost moved to stop him. As it did, Martin made his escape, running down the stairs and fleeing into the street. He was later found unconscious on the footpath, and after he was revived he told a passing policeman that he had seen an apparition, which he described as that of a white-faced man, his mouth agape in evil.

PANICKED INTO DEATH

The policeman was highly sceptical about the sailor's claims, but agreed to accompany Martin into the house to find his friend. When they arrived, they found Blunden's broken body sprawled on the basement stairs. His neck had been broken, and his eyes bulged in eternal horror. Apparently he had been so panicked by whatever he had seen that he had fallen down the stairs to his death. In the years since, many people have tried to explain the events inside 50 Berkeley Square, but no one has yet been able to offer convincing proof that the disasters that befell Warboys, the maid, Lord Lyttleton, the sailors and the others were not the work of some supernatural force.

In 1924, however, author Charles Harper wrote in his book, *Haunted Houses*, that one of the owners of the house, a Mr Du Pre, kept his mentally retarded brother imprisoned in the house. Mr Harper claims that the wretched lunatic was terribly violent, and given to frenzied bouts of sobbing and anger, in which he would throw objects about and scream with rage.

However, Harper's theory does not explain why the witnesses were never able to fully describe the monstrosity they had all seen. Nor does it explain why the house was so often put up for let. After all, who in their right mind would move into a house that came complete with a demented madman as a permanent guest in the upstairs room? Moreover, if both Sir Robert and Lord Lyttleton had shot at this insane prisoner, why was no blood ever found, let alone a body? And lastly, could any human being, no matter how deranged, literally frighten to death a knight of the realm and two of Her Majesty's servicemen? One can only answer with a resounding, 'No'.

Whatever strange disturbances occurred inside 50 Berkeley Square is a mystery which lasts to this very day. Fortunately for the new tenants, there have been no supernatural incidents reported at the site for many years.

BORLEY RECTORY

That is not the case with the Borley Rectory, with good reason called 'the most haunted house in England'. The Rectory, which lies some 60 miles north-east of London in the county of Essex, is a grotesque-looking building, isolated from surrounding houses by a lonely country road. The house, a gloomy red-brick monstrosity, has always had an eerie aura about it, and visitors down through the years have remarked forlorn appearance.

The Rectory was said to have been h time it was built, in 1863, and dow' decades everyone who ever lived in of visitors have all claimed that some work inside.

Borley Rectory is rightly called the most haunted house in England. Over the years, many residents have fled from it in mortal fear.

A HAUNTED SITE

The first occupants were the Revd. Henry Bull, who built it, and his wife and family. Even when they moved in, all were aware of the local legend that a monastery had once occupied the site, and that a monk had tried to elope with a nun from a nearby convent at Bures. According to the story, the ill-fated lovers were captured soon after they fled. The monk was hanged, and the nun bricked up alive inside one of the walls. Every 28

July, it was said, the lonely figure of a nun could be seen almost gliding along a path, forever searching for her long-dead lover. All four of the reverend's daughters saw the nun-like figure on 28 July 1900, and tried to speak with her. The apparition simply vanished into thin air. Numerous other people, including a local headmaster, also claimed to have seen the nun.

When the Revd Bull died in 1892 the Rectory was taken over by his only son, the Revd Harry Bull, who had also seen the nun. But there were many other mysterious intruders besides her. On many occasions, Harry Bull heard bells ringing with no possible earthly explanation, and he claimed to have seen and heard a phantom coach with horses. Once, he claimed to have seen the vehicle driven by two headless horsemen! Before his death in 1927 he told many people that he had no doubts that the place was indeed haunted.

For almost 12 months following his death, the Rectory remained vacant, largely because no fewer than 12 clergymen turned down the post and local folks avoided it as soon as nightfall approached. It was not until the Revd Eric Smith and his wife, both avowed non-believers in the paranormal, moved in in 1928 that the lights burned again inside the Borley Rectory. But soon after they arrived, their resolve weakened. They, too, began to see and hear strange, unexplainable things: Mrs Smith reported seeing the phantom coach and horses; lights inside the house would flick off and on by themselves; bells rang out; mysterious footsteps were heard. And on one occasion, Revd Smith said he heard a woman groan, then listened as she exclaimed: 'Don't, Carlos, don't!'

BLACK SHAPES

They also claimed to have seen black shapes wandering about the rooms and, on one occasion, they said that they saw the ghost of Revd Harry Bull! This is an astounding fact because sometime before his death, Harry said if he was not happy with his successor, he would come back to haunt the place.

The frightened couple finally decided that they had better get some professional help in to investigate the spooky occurrences, and soon famed ghost hunter Harry Price arrived on the scene to examine the paranormal happenings. Price quickly found volumes of evidence to support the Smiths' claims, including unexplained footsteps in the snow, terrified animals, knocks on doors and walls, objects flying about the rooms. Despite his assurances – or maybe because of them – that they were not imagining things, the Smiths had finally endured enough. One year after the sceptical couple first moved in, they were gone. But the ghosts remained!

In 1930, Revd Lionel Foyster and his wife Marianne arrived at Borley Rectory, and for the next five years, until they too left in panic, the hauntings not only continued, but increased in dramatic frenzy. Eerie messages – begging for 'Mass' and 'Prayers' – were found scrawled on pieces of paper and walls; Marianne was savagely struck across the eye by some invisible force; their three-year- old daughter, Adelaide, was locked in a room that had no key; objects were tossed violently around the rooms; bottles materialized from thin air, then vanished as they had appeared. Many of these paranormal phenomena occurred in the presence of witnesses, including a Justice of the Peace, a military officer and numerous other reliable spectators.

CONTINUED INVESTIGATIONS

Like the others before them, the Foysters eventually moved out and the Rectory was again vacant until 1937, when Harry Price decided to lease the site for 12 months so that he could continue his investigation into the dramatic hauntings. During

The church at Borley is said to have been haunted from when it was built, 130 years ago.

the first few nights, he and a companion, Ellic Howe, drew circles in chalk around the bases of many movable objects in the Rectory. Each morning, the objects had somehow moved!

Gradually, Price gathered together a large team of investigators – at one stage there were 40 in all – who set up various experiments to try and record the ghosts' movements. This was to no avail, but in subsequent seances, Harry Bull appeared and told medium S.H. Glanville that the bodies of the monk and the nun had been buried on the site. In March 1938, another medium was told that the Rectory would burn to the ground that very evening, and that the hauntings would cease. Nothing happened, but it's interesting to note that indeed the place was gutted by fire in February 1939. By that time, Captain W.H. Gregson had owned the house for just three months. He was going through some books when a stack of them accidentally fell over, knocking an oil lamp to the ground.

SPOOKY REMAINS

However, shortly before the disaster, Revd Canon W.J. Phythian-Adams, who had recently read Price's book about the Rectory, discovered that a young French woman had been murdered at the site and that her remains were buried there sometime in the 17th or 18th century. At his suggestion, Price and his team excavated the cellar and found the remains of a long-departed young woman!

Towards the end of 1939, Dr A.J. Robertson organized yet another team of investigators to pore over the burned out remains of the Rectory. For the next five years, he and his team recorded more strange occurrences including inexplicable noises and rappings, stones thrown by an invisible hand, temperature changes which could not be accounted for by the prevailing weather and sightings of an eerie, incandescent patch.

Similarly, in recent years other reliable witnesses, including a headmistress, another rector and a Sunday school teacher, have all reported seeing or hearing evidence of the paranormal at the site. Organ music has been heard by many coming from inside the church, which is empty and locked; the nun has been sighted several times. One witness, who saw a female apparition in 1951, described the woman as sad and wearing a black hood, a white collar, a gold bodice and a long black skirt. Another witness, Peter Rowe, a retired official from the Bank of England, saw the nun running past the gate towards the former garden. Sightings of her have come as recently as the 1970s.

PECULIAR SMELLS

Incredibly, even though the Rectory itself is no longer still standing, peculiar smells can still be noticed emanating from where it once sat and the sound of furniture being moved about can also be heard. Others have reported hearing plates being smashed, while others have heard voices. The ghosts of Borley Rectory, it seems, are still at play.

Ghost hunters and researchers have flocked to the site at Borley Rectory, looking for evidence of the paranormal.

A GHOST IN FLIGHT

Most encounters with ghosts occur in haunted houses or castles, but there is one remarkable story concerning a haunted passenger plane. This state-of-the-art commercial jet flew for many months with a very unusual passenger on board.

The ghost of Tri-Star 318 is as bizarre an apparition as anything to be found in the fog-cloaked graveyards or Gothic castles of England and France. Indeed, even a US government agency was unable to solve the mystery or explain what it was that many experienced airline crews had seen and heard. The first warning that something was amiss aboard Tri-Star 318 came in 1973, when Fay Merryweather, a senior stewardess of several years' experience and a respected member of the flight crew, was walking back towards the rear of the Eastern Airlines plane to prepare the lunch for the 180 passengers fleeing the snow of New York for the sun-baked beaches of Florida. But as she walked back into the galley to begin heating the food, she remembers feeling something – or someone – watching her every movement. She remembers feeling a little uneasy, then suddenly, she turned her eyes and saw it – the reflection of a face staring at her from the tinted glass door of the in-flight oven.

Merryweather remembered being shocked, but when she looked closer at the vision, she was somehow not frightened. The face wasn't some grotesque, contorted image. Instead, it was the one that looked worried! Then, the mouth began to move, but no sound came. The stewardess got the impression that it was trying to warn her about something. Not knowing what to do, she quickly but calmly walked up the cabin aisle to the cockpit, carefully ensuring she did not arouse the suspicion of her passengers, and informed the flight engineer of the strange sighting.

Puzzled, because he knew Merryweather to be an experienced flier and not one prone to fanciful hallucinations, the officer left the cockpit and his bank of instruments and followed her back to the galley to take a look himself. When he looked into the oven door, not only was the disembodied face still there – but the startled engineer recognized it! It was Don Repo, a former colleague who had died 12 months earlier in a tragic plane crash that occurred over the Florida Everglades! As both stared at the image in disbelief, they heard it whisper: 'Beware! Beware! Fire in the jet!' Strangely, there was nothing amiss on board the Tri-Star that day, but the ominous warning was to come true three months later on another Eastern Airlines flight.

A PUZZLING APPARITION

The puzzling apparition forced officials and Eastern Airlines crew members to recall that devastating night some months earlier, when tragedy struck the airline. Rep, an engineer, and pilot Bob Loft were killed along with more than 100 passengers while on the same run between New York and Florida on the night of 29 December 1972. The plane was a new Lockheed L-1011, or Tri-Star, the pride of the Eastern fleet and one of the most sophisticated planes then plying the skies over America. It was the first of the new generation of wide-body 'jumbo jets' to crash. The death toll at the time was the highest of any one-plane accident in United States' civil aviation history, and its downing made headlines around the world.

According to the lengthy, official investigation into the horrible crash of Flight 401, the trip had been routine for most of the way. Indeed, with Miami in sight, Captain Loft had announced cheerfully to his passengers and crew: 'Welcome to sunny Miami', as the plane passed over the city. 'The temperature is in the low 70s, and it's beautiful out there tonight.'

But as Captain Loft made the remarks, Repo went through the pre-landing motions, activating the sign instructing passengers to fasten their seat belts, then flicking the switch which would lower the wheels. It was then that the cockpit crew noticed that the square green light on the control panel which should have indicated that the nose wheel was locked and secured into position had failed to come on.

Captain Loft immediately put the Tri-Star on automatic pilot to circle, while Repo scurried to an observation point to see whether or not the nose gear had activated. As he did, Loft then decided to see if the problem was not merely a faulty indicator light. The captain guessed, correctly as it turned out, that the nose wheel was all right and locked into position and that the light was faulty. However, he still called off the landing and flew away from other airport traffic to make certain. After that, everything seemed to go wrong. Tragically, Captain Loft somehow bumped the automatic pilot switch into the 'off' position while he continued to check his panel – and neither he nor Repo realized the error until the plane was plummeting into a swamp.

An Eastern Airlines Tri-Star . . . identical to the one that became known as a ghost plane.

There was nothing they could do, because unavoidable disaster was just seconds away. The left wingtip hit first, and the jet ploughed into the murky waters of the Everglades, leaving 101 people dead, and 75 lucky survivors. Initially, both Repo and Loft survived the horrific crash. Unfortunately, Loft died about 60 minutes later, still trapped inside the doomed cockpit, while Repo, who paramedics say seemed terribly angry when they pulled him from the smoking wreckage, lingered for more than a day before finally succumbing to his extensive injuries.

DEATH COMES CALLING

Angelo Donadeo, an Eastern Airlines technical specialist on L-1011 aircraft, was returning to Miami that night from a trouble-shooting assignment in New York and remembers it well. Although he was a passenger, he rode in the cockpit with Loft, Repo and co-pilot A. Stockstill, who was also killed. 'That wasn't my first brush with death,' Donadeo recalled many years later. 'I was wounded in World War Two when the ship I was on was hit by a kamikaze. I had first, second and third degree burns all over my body. That doesn't haunt me either. I don't see any reason to worry about what fate has brought. I don't question what the Lord does.' According to the records, Flight 401 flew into the ground just 18 minutes before midnight, crashing into the Everglades 18 miles north-west of the airport.

A survivor, Richard Micale, told local reporters that it had all happened so quickly. 'I remember thinking "Shit! The plane's crashing," and before I got finished thinking it, it was over. You could hear the cry of death. Funny how people scream for God at a time like that. I probably did too, I'm sure.'

STUNNING STORIES

Witnesses recall that there was a huge flash of flame as two fuel tanks burst open, sending burning bodies and debris flying into the air and into the alligator-infested waters. Richard Marquis, a carpet-layer, was out that night on his airboat catching frogs with a friend, Ray Dickens. They headed towards the flash, and saw the lights of rescue helicopters, circling and searching over the black lagoon.

The scattered wreckage of Flight 401 which went down on a landing approach outside Miami International Airport in December 1972: months later strange events began.

They were much too far to the east and south, Marquis recalled, so he began to wave his headlamp in circles, guiding the rescue pilots to the crash site. Afterwards, he and his friend spent most of the night taking doctors and paramedics to the injured, and the injured to the levee where the helicopters were landing to whisk them away to the nearest hospitals.

Following the lengthy investigation, which took several weeks, maintenance crews managed to salvage parts of the doomed airliner, which were then installed into other Tri-Star craft. The galley was installed into Tri-Star 318, where stewardess Merryweather and the flight engineer encountered Repo's ghost. Although his warning of a fire never eventuated on that flight to Florida, it did come true three months later, when the plane was forced to turn back with engine trouble on a trip from Mexico to New York.

Repairs were ordered and, when completed, the Tri-Star was sent up on a routine test flight to check the servicing. Just as the pilot edged the nose into the air, one of the engines suddenly burst into flames. The official report issued some weeks later found that if it had not been for the experience and professionalism of the crew, the plane would have crashed.

THE CAPTAIN'S GHOST

Later, on another flight, Captain Loft's ghost was sighted. The plane was filled with Eastern Airlines' staff, returning to their home base in Florida from various destinations around the United States. Among those aboard was an off-duty pilot and a senior airline executive, who sat next to each other. Not long into the flight, the two men began chatting, and when the executive turned to look at his fellow passenger, he recoiled in horror – for sitting next to him was Captain Loft, who had been dead for more than 12 months! (Oddly, the third member of the flight crew of flight 401, First Officer Stockstill, was never seen.) The executive let out a scream, and a host of fellow workers and stewardesses rushed to his aid. They found him ashen and shaking – and the seat next to him very much empty. A short while later on yet another flight, Captain Loft appeared again, still dressed in his captain's uniform, sitting in the first class section of the plane. A stewardess came over to him, and asked why he did not appear on her passenger list. When he didn't reply, she went to see the captain, who accompanied her back to the first class cabin. He immediately recognized Loft, who then suddenly vanished into thin air right before their eyes.

There were several more sightings of the doomed fliers. A stewardess on another flight saw Repo's face appear on a luggage locker, while another spotted Loft near the bulkhead. In all, there were more than 20 sightings. One of the last came in

1974, when a pilot was conducting his routine pre-take-off check for a flight to Georgia.

As he inspected the complex bank of dials before him, the face of Dan Repo appeared. But this time, there were no warnings of near-disasters. Instead, the face whispered that he had already made the inspection, then added: 'There will never be another crash on an L-1011. We will not let it happen.' The voice had used the Lockheed serial number of the Tri-Star jet.

Still others claim to have had eerie encounters with the dead aviators. Some say they heard Repo's voice coming in over the public address system, while a few passengers say they felt inexplicable sudden rushes of cold air. During one haunting, in which Repo appeared yet again in the galley, he repaired an oven that had a circuit dangerously close to overloading. When the engineer assigned to the flight came to investigate the problem, he told the stunned air stewardess that he was the only engineer on the plane. Later, she looked up Repo's photo from his employment file and positively identified him as the man who had fixed the errant oven.

By this time the rash of apparitions had begun to worry crew members, but Eastern Airlines executives remained sceptical. Also, they didn't want the ghost stories made public, for fear that they could seriously erode the airline's passenger business. Those who reported seeing or hearing either Repo or Captain Loft were often urged to see a company psychiatrist, which was seen as the stage before getting fired. Eventually, however, as the number of sightings grew, Eastern management, which had no idea what could be causing the hauntings, called in an employee with devout religious leanings, and asked his advice. The man knew there could be just one way to rid the Tri-Star of its high-flying ghosts – an exorcism, which he did by splashing holy water about the plane. It worked, because the ghosts of Repo and Loft were never seen again. They were finally at rest

– or so it seemed. Shortly afterwards, details of the sightings were forwarded to the Flight Safety Foundation, which oversees airline safety in the United States. Its report, issued several weeks later, concluded: 'The reports were given by experienced and trustworthy pilots and crew. We consider them significant. The appearance of the dead flight engineer in the galley door was confirmed by the flight engineer. Later, records at the Federal Aviation Agency record the fire which broke out in that same aircraft. We published reports of the ghost sightings in our safety bulletin issued to airlines in 1974.'

But the Flight Safety Foundation never offered an explanation of the eerie apparitions, and to this day the hauntings remain a complete mystery.

Interestingly, some locals also claim to have seen the ghosts of some of those who died on Flight 401 roaming the Everglades late at night. Sadie Messina, whose husband was aboard the doomed craft, had a terrible premonition as she waited at the gate for the plane that would never arrive. 'My husband always had a distinctive little whistle, a code whistle,' she said.

'When I heard that whistle, I knew he was home. We were waiting at the gate, my two sons and I, and I heard his whistle. It sounded like he was right behind me. I turned around to look, but, of course, he wasn't there.' Sadie swears she heard the whistle at precisely the time Flight 401 crashed. Her husband, Rosario Messina, was among the dead.

Further, a secluded strip of land just outside Miami, which was once targeted to house the world's largest airport, is also said to be home to Don Repo's ghost. In 1969, it was envisioned as a massive hub for SSTs and 747s, but today it is a windswept piece of prairie, used for training airline pilots. But locals say that they have had several reports of his ghost in the area!

The bizarre hauntings remain a mystery to this very day.

American actor Ernest Borgnine,
dressed as an airline pilot, for his role in the telefilm
The Ghost of Flight 401, *January 1978.*

HAUNTED U-BOAT

It was the ghost from which there was no escape, the ghost that had its victims trapped – the ghost of U-boat 65. For the submariners in the German navy, a posting onto that submarine was almost as terrifying as coming under attack from the enemy.

Almost two years into the Great War, the battlefields of France and Belgium were literally running red with blood. Hundreds of thousands of young men were dying, an entire generation consigned to the mud and mayhem of trench warfare along the Western Front. The conflagration was so evenly matched that victories were measured in mere yards. Neither side could muster the reserves for that one decisive thrust to punch through the other's defences, and the war developed into a grotesque stalemate – except that in this case, the pawns were the young men of England, Germany and France.

The only breakthrough in the war, it seemed, might come at sea where, by the summer of 1916, the Kaiser's navy, led by the wolf packs of U-boat submarines, was beginning to take a heavy toll on British shipping. Hundreds of thousands of tons were consigned to the bottom of the seas by the fast-moving U-boats. Particularly hard hit was the British merchant fleet, which carried supplies vital to the war effort in Europe.

The Kaiser and his navy warlords were convinced that this was the way to break the back of the British bulldog and so, with the war two years old, Germany was devoting much of its total war effort to producing more and more submarines to press the attack. That year, among the many U-boats which came down the assembly line ready for British blood was UB65, which would go down in naval lore as the host to at least one ghost, and the scene of many disturbing and tragic occurrences. Indeed, UB65 became so infamous, that even as the war raged on, its panic-stricken crew grew increasingly reluctant to sail on her.

Even before she was launched, the 'Iron Coffin' as she became known, seemed to attract disaster. She was built to join a fleet of submarines prowling off the Flemish coastline, gorging on the slow, heavily laden ships crossing back and forward across the English Channel. But it seemed that everything that could go wrong during construction, did.

A HORRIFYING END

Not even seven days into her construction, as the hull was being laid, the first tragedy struck. As workers poured over the site, a giant girder hovering overhead on chains suddenly broke free, plunging into the hull. A hapless worker was horribly crushed under its massive weight, and lay there, in agony, for over an hour while frantic mates tried to rescue him. Tragically, he died just as the huge weight was finally lifted off him. An inquiry into the accident found there had been no faults in the chains used to hoist the girder, and officials were mystified as to what could have caused it to snap free.

Less than two months later, there was a second, more alarming tragedy. Three engineers who were assigned to the U-boat's engine room to test the submarine's dry-cell batteries, were overcome by deadly chloride fumes. They died before anyone could rescue them and drag them into the fresh air. No one ever determined why the batteries leaked the toxic fumes.

When the Great War became bogged down on bloody battlefields, the Germans deployed more of their dreaded U-boats.

Thankfully, there were no more mysterious incidents during the remaining construction and shortly afterwards UB65 set sail for sea trials. But whatever dogged the boat seemed to follow it out of port because it quickly ran into a fierce Channel storm, and one hapless sailor was washed overboard to his death when the vessel came up to test her stability on the surface during rough seas.

After the man went overboard, the captain ordered the U-boat to dive. As she did, a ballast tank sprang a leak, flooding the dry-cell batteries with sea water and filling the engine room with the same deadly gas that had already claimed three lives while the boat was still on the slipway. After 12 nerve-racking hours the crew finally managed to get the ship to surface, where they flung open the hatches and breathed clean air. Amazingly, no one was killed, and the bedevilled craft limped back to Germany for repairs.

After several days, the U-boat was again readied for sea and her first on-line patrol. But as a battery of torpedoes was being placed on board, a warhead suddenly exploded, killing the second officer and badly wounding several others. Yet again, an inquiry was conducted, but no explanation for the explosion was ever found. In the meantime, the second officer was buried, and another round of repairs made to the jinxed vessel. Her jittery crew, already worried about the U-boat's growing reputation for being accursed, were given a few days' much-needed shore leave to calm their shattered nerves before setting out on their first active patrol.

A GHASTLY APPARITION

Yet just moments before she was set to leave port, another bizarre incident occurred – this time, a panicked sailor swore he had seen the apparition of the dead second officer. 'Herr

Kapitan!' he blurted. 'The dead officer is on board!' The captain, of course, refused to take the report seriously, believing the sailor had had too much to drink during his shore leave. However, even the stoic skipper was a little taken aback when a second member of his crew also claimed to have seen the ghost of the second officer coming casually up the gangplank! The seaman was sobbing from fear when he told the captain that the apparition had walked aboard, strolled up to the bow, then looked out at the inviting sea. He then vanished into thin air.

That two crew members had reported seeing the dead officer gave the captain some reason for pause, but nevertheless he knew his duty lay at sea and in sinking British ships. UB65 had some early successes on its maiden voyage, sinking three Allied merchant ships in quick succession. However, the rumours of the unwanted ghost had spread through the crew like wildfire, and their celebration over any direct hits was tempered by their belief that their vessel was haunted.

STARTLED SAILORS

Indeed, there was almost full-scale panic after UB65 recorded its second kill, when startled sailors in the engine room saw the dead officer observing the instrument panel as he had done in the trial voyage. By the time the submarine returned to base, rumours of its ghostly visitor were already spreading throughout the entire U-boat armada. The captain did his best to dispel the talk, claiming it was all poppycock, fearing that the ghost tales would only further erode the morale of the 34-man crew. But in their hearts, the men of UB65 knew something was terribly amiss with their craft.

Then in January 1918, as the war dragged ever closer to its inevitable conclusion, even the captain could no longer dismiss the sightings as the rantings of some foolhardy seamen – for he, too, saw the apparition! It came as the U-boat was prowling in the Channel off Portland Bill. Because the weather was so foul and the seas extremely rough, the captain ordered the craft

U-boat 65 was forced to limp back to harbour after another mysterious disaster. The submarine was bedevilled by tragedy and death.

to surface. After breaking the surface, a lookout stationed on the starboard side was scanning the stormy horizon. He turned to look to port, when suddenly he spotted an officer standing on the deck, which heaved under the growing fury of the waves. At first, the crewman thought the officer foolhardy for taking such a risk, but then realized that all the hatches were still battened down, bar the one from which he himself had climbed onto the deck. He knew no one could have come up through there without him immediately spotting him.

ALL-OUT PANIC

Suddenly, the crewman got a full look at the officer – and his face went white as the blood drained from it. There standing in front of him was the second officer, who had been buried with full honours back at home base. When he finally summoned the courage to move, the terrified seamen screamed to his shipmates that the ghost was on the boat. Below deck, the crew was close to all-out panic, and the captain had to act immediately lest a hysterical sailor put all their lives in jeopardy. He raced up the ladder, fully expecting to see nothing save a panicked crewman, when he, too, saw his dead comrade, his face a grotesque distortion. Seconds later, the ghost vanished, as if blown into the raging swell by the strong winds.

By the time the U-boat returned to port, navy authorities were already waiting. They were determined to get to the bottom of the mystery, fearing that the morale of the crew was so low that another disaster was just waiting to happen. With intense secrecy, each and every man assigned to UB65 was interviewed by a panel of high ranking officers.

The reader must remember that U-boat crews were among the most reliable and hardiest in the navy. They were subjected to long periods of confinement deep below the ocean surface, and had to withstand hours of nerve-racking pursuit by Allied destroyers. It was a fact that a submariner had only a 50-50 chance of ever returning from his mission, and that on a man-for-man basis, the U-boat force suffered the highest casualties of the war. So when these brave, innately fearless men, told navy officials that they were terrified of returning to their craft because of ghosts, then their story could not simply be dismissed as irrational rantings. And it wasn't. Although the Kaiser's sea lords could never admit to having a haunted ship – one could imagine the widespread effect on morale that would have on their other crews – they found the stories about the ghost of the dead second officer too convincing to simply laugh off or dismiss as the talk of overwrought sailors. Instead, they decided to break up the crew of UB65, sending some to other submarines and others to destroyers.

But that still left the problem of what to do with the vessel itself. Eventually, the U-boat was decommissioned at the port of Bruges, in Belgium, and a Lutheran pastor was asked to perform the ancient Christian rite of exorcism! In surely what must be one of the most incredible wartime scenes ever, a Belgian civilian was taken on board while German officers watched with a mixture of fascination and dread. Once the exorcism was completed, everyone breathed a sigh of relief.

A new crew and captain were assigned to the 'cleansed' ship, and it was business as usual for the next few weeks. The new skipper, a stern disciplinarian who scoffed at the stories of dead men walking the ship, warned his crew that he would not tolerate any renewed tales of ghosts or goblins. For the next two missions, it appeared as if everything was back to normal. There had been no sightings and no inexplicable accidents. But in May 1918, the ghost appeared again.

During the long voyage, in which UB65 was ordered to patrol the sea lanes off the Spanish coast as well as the English Channel, the dead officer was seen no fewer than three times. One of those who saw the ghost was the petty officer, who swore to God that he saw the man walk through a solid iron bulkhead and pass into the engine room! Another man, a torpedo handler, claimed the ghost visited him several times at night. The terrified soul became so disorientated that when the submarine surfaced to recharge its batteries, he leaped off the deck to his death in the seas.

On its final voyage – during July 1918, just four months before the Armistice was signed and peace returned to a ravaged Europe – the UB65 was spotted by an American submarine resting like a sitting duck on the surface. No one knows why. It was 10 July. The American sailors, who couldn't believe their good fortune, quickly armed their torpedoes and prepared to fire. But just before they did, the UB65 suddenly exploded, sending the remains of metal and men spewing out over a wide range of ocean.

Within seconds, all that remained of the submarine and her crew was a heavy oil slick and scattered debris. No one aboard the American submarine ever gave the order to fire, and the crew swears no one launched a torpedo. What happened? To this day, no one knows. But it seemed a fitting, if bloody, end to the story of the haunted ship, which took its most enigmatic secret with it to its watery grave.

*Just four months before the Armistice was signed, U-boat 65
suddenly exploded – killing everyone aboard.*

GHOST SHIP

Nothing strikes fear into a sailor as much as the sighting of a dreaded ghost ship, condemned to sail the world's oceans for all eternity. And of all the tales of accursed ships, none has remained as mysterious or as terrifying as that of the Flying Dutchman.

The *Flying Dutchman*, which was immortalized by the German writer Heinrich Heine and composer Richard Wagner in his opera, *Der Fliegende Hollander*, many years later, was a 17th-century brig that plied the sea lanes between Holland and the East Indies, at the centre of the lucrative spice trade. The full story of the ship's tortured journey through time was first recounted by the French writer, Auguste Jal, in about 1832.

In his book, Jal wrote that the vessel was rounding the Cape of Good Hope on its way to the East Indies, when it was struck by a frightful storm. The Dutch sea captain, a greedy, ill-tempered tyrant who was infamous for his cruelty, refused to listen to the pleas of his panicked crew who begged him to turn back for home lest the ship sink. But the captain only laughed at them and their terror, and he began singing blasphemous songs and drinking beer. As the raging storm worsened, it tore the sails and snapped the masts, leaving the *Flying Dutchman* completely at its mercy. But still the captain, now further emboldened by drink, laughed and ridiculed his terrified crew.

Then suddenly, at the height of the tempest, the clouds began to part, and a ghostly presence, said in Jal's account to have been God himself, appeared on the quarter deck for all to see. The crew were stricken with fright, but the evil captain began to blaspheme the presence when it offered safety.

'Who wants a peaceful passage?' the captain shouted. 'I don't. I'm asking nothing from you, so clear out of this unless you want your brains blown out.'

According to Jal, the ghostly presence just shrugged its shoulders, so the captain grabbed a pistol and fired a bullet into the spectre. But instead, the gun misfired, injuring the captain's hand. Angrily, he rushed towards the apparition, and went to strike it. But his arm went limp, as if paralysed. In his wild rage, the Captain began to curse and blaspheme even more 'and called the presence all sorts of terrible names'.

By now, the apparition had had enough and spoke gravely: 'From now on, you are accursed, condemned to sail forever. For you shall be the evil spirit of the sea. You will be allowed no anchorage or port of any kind. You shall have neither beer nor tobacco. Gall shall be your drink and red hot iron your meat. Of your crew, your cabin boy alone shall remain with you; horns shall grow out of his forehead, and he shall have the muzzle of a tiger and skin tougher than that of a dogfish.

'It shall ever be your watch, and when you wish, you will not be able to sleep, for directly you close your eyes, a sword shall pierce your body. And since it is your delight to torment sailors, you shall torment them. For you shall be the evil spirit of the sea. You shall travel all latitudes without rest, and your ship shall bring misfortune to all who sight her… And on the day of atonement, the Devil shall claim you.'

Then the presence vanished, leaving the captain alone, save for his cabin boy, who by now had the horns and the face of a tiger. From that moment on, Jal wrote, the *Flying Dutchman* was the bane of the seven seas, forever doomed to its miserable existence.

AN INFAMOUS INDIVIDUAL

Strangely, Jal never names the malicious and heretical captain, but history indicates that it may have been Cornelius Vanderdecken, who apparently had the same vile temper and cruel demeanour as that attributed to the unnamed skipper. Moreover, Vanderdecken frequently sailed the seas off Africa, and was known to pass the Cape of Good Hope every four to six months. He was also notoriously greedy, and never let the safety of his crew stand in the way of making good time. And he was notorious for his blasphemous language.

Likewise, another Dutch captain, Bernard Fokke, has also

been linked with the legend of the doomed ship. Like Vanderdecken, Fokke, too, was a foul-mouthed despot, who often made the passage between Holland and the East Indies in 90 days, regardless of the weather or the mutterings of his crew. Interestingly, Fokke was also accused of making a pact with the Devil to ensure his trips were speedy. Eventually, there was a falling out between the two, and Fokke was said to have been damned for all eternity.

The crew of a whaling ship, the Orkney Belle*, saw the* Dutchman *off the frigid seas of Iceland.*

Of course, it doesn't really matter which of the two brutes was at the helm of the *Fying Dutchman*. After all, say the sceptics, the very idea of a ship being condemned by God or the Devil is proof enough that the entire legend is nothing but a joke or a story to frighten young children. But upon further examination, it becomes clear that while Jal must have embellished the story, there is ample evidence to suggest that there is much more to the *Flying Dutchman* story than just myth. It cannot simply be dismissed - because a vessel matching its description has been seen by sailors all over the world, and many of those ships which have come into contact with it have been hit by a bizarre spate of mysterious mishaps.

Indeed, it was once even seen by the future King of England! In July 1881, Prince George, who would later become King George V, was serving as a midshipman aboard   HMS *Inconstant*, a heavily armed frigate and one of Her Majesty's most modern ships.

On 11 July, his log would recount, the ship was sailing between Melbourne and Sydney when suddenly he and 12 other crew members noticed an eerie light coming from over the horizon.

In his private journal, the Prince wrote: 'At 4 a.m. the "Flying Dutchman" crossed our bows. A strange red light, as of a phantom ship all aglow, in the midst of which light the mast, spars and sails of a brig two hundred yards distant stood out in strong relief as she come up on port bow. The look-out man on the forecastle reported her as close on the port bow, where also the officer of the watch from the bridge clearly saw her, as did the quarterdeck midshipman, who was sent forward at once to the forecastle; but on arriving there, no vestige nor any sign whatever of any material ship was to be seen either near or right away to the horizon, the night being clear and calm. Thirteen persons saw her.'

UNEXPLAINED TRAGEDIES

Incredibly, the so-called 'curse' of the *Flying Dutchman* soon followed. The seaman who had first reported seeing the vessel fell from the top mast to his death later that very same day. Then, a few days later, the Admiral of the Fleet also died, and many of the crewmen became gravely ill. It was never fully explained why.

There have been numerous other sightings recorded throughout the years. A full 15 years before the young Prince reported seeing the haunted ship, those aboard the American vessel, the *General Grant*, had an equally horrible encounter with the doomed Dutchman. In early May 1866, the *General Grant* left port in Melbourne for the long voyage to England. Everything seemed routine for the first two weeks, until the winds slackened, sending the *Grant* drifting helplessly away from the normal shipping lanes. On 13 May, the ship was pulled by the currents towards Auckland Island, a dismal, rocky outcrop in the middle of nowhere. The *Grant* was driven along the coastline until it was eventually forced into a huge cave. Its masts scraped along the top of the cavern, sending a shower of rocks crashing onto its deck. Almost miraculously, no-one was injured, but the seafarers' ordeal wasn't over yet.

Because of its position, the cave was subjected to sudden onrushes of waves, which forced the *Grant* deeper and deeper into its bowels. Eventually, the masts became so wedged that one of them was forced through the hull.

The *Grant* began to take on water and, in a panic, some of the 46 passengers dived overboard to their deaths.

Those who remained joined the crew in frantically lowering three lifeboats. Unfortunately, one of the lifeboats was then dashed against the rocks and broke up. All but three of the 40 people aboard were killed. Those in the other two boats, 14 in all, were luckier. They made it out of the cavern, and decided to row towards nearby Disappointment Island.

After a break, they continued their slow journey to the Auckland Islands, where they lived a desperate existence for more than 18 months until they were rescued by another vessel.

According to accounts of the time, the *General Grant* was actually lured to disaster by the spectre of the *Flying Dutchman*. As the ship drifted helplessly in the still winds another ship, said to be the *Dutchman*, suddenly appeared on the horizon and led the *Grant* to its watery grave.

The crew of the whaling steamer *Orkney Belle* also had an eerie experience. This one took place in January 1911, as the *Orkney Belle* ploughed through the frigid seas off the coast of Iceland.

A second mate later recounted the sighting to the London *Daily News*: 'The captain and I were on the bridge and a thin mist swirled over everything. Suddenly, this thin mist thinned out… to our mutual horror and surprise, a sailing vessel loomed up virtually head on.

'I rammed the helm hard aport and we seemed to escape the collision by a hair's breadth. Then, with startling suddenness, old Anderson, the carpenter, bawled out: 'The Flying Dutchman'.

'The captain and I scoffed at him, for we thought that oft-fabled ship existed in the minds of only superstitious sailors.

'As the strange vessel slowly slid alongside within a stone's throw, we noticed with amazement that her sails were billowing, yet there was no wind at all. She was a replica of a barque I once saw in a naval museum. Meantime, practically all the crew rushed to the ship's side, some in terror, but unable to resist their curiosity. Not a soul was to be seen aboard this strange vessel, not a ripple did her bows make.

'Then, like a silver bell, so sweet was the tone, three bells sounded, as if from the bows of the phantom ship, and as if in

King George was one of the many distinguished persons who have come across the haunted vessel.

answer to a signal, the craft heeled to starboard and disappeared into the fog…'

A GHOSTLY APPARITION

The second mate's story echoes that of dozens of others, some of whom claim to have seen the ghostly ship well into the 20th century, still sailing aimlessly across the seven seas.

In January 1923, its apparition appeared off the Cape of Good Hope and was seen by at least four veteran seamen. One of them, N.K. Stone, later wrote of the encounter: 'At about 0.15 a.m., we noticed a strange "light" on the port bow… it was a very dark night, overcast, with no moon. We looked at this through binoculars and the ship's telescope, and made out what appeared to be the hull of a sailing ship, luminous, with no distinct masts carrying bare yards, also luminous; no sails were visible, but there was a luminous haze between the masts.

'There were no navigation lights, and she appeared to be coming close to us and at the same speed as ourselves.

'When first sighted, she was about two to three miles away, and when she was about a half-mile of us, she suddenly disappeared. There were four witnesses of this spectacle, myself, the second officer, a cadet, the helmsman and myself. I shall never forget the second officer's startled expressions – "My God, Stone, it's a ghost ship".'

Later, during World War Two, there were numerous sightings, and even Germany's Grand Admiral Karl Donitz admitted 'that certain of my U-boat crews claimed they saw the *Flying Dutchman* or some other so-called phantom ship on their tours of duty east of Suez. When they returned to their base, the men said they preferred facing the combined strength of Allied warships in the North Atlantic to knowing the terror a second time of being confronted by a phantom vessel.' Even Hitler's 'supermen' were afraid of ghosts!

Incredibly, the *Flying Dutchman* has also been seen by people fortunate enough to be on dry land when the eerie apparition appeared. In 1939, more than 100 startled swimmers at South Africa's Glencairn Beach in False Bay, near the Cape of Good Hope, claimed to have seen the *Dutchman* at full sail gliding gently across the water, even though there was no discernible wind that day. The stunned bathers were mystified at the sight, but when it suddenly vanished, they were absolutely baffled.

Three years later, this time near Cape Town, a South African family was relaxing on the terrace of their ocean-front home when they watched as an old sailing ship passed by them. All four of them later said that they viewed the ship for more than 15 minutes, until it vanished, leaving behind only a bright glow in its wake.

Since then, there has been at least one more sighting. In 1957, again off the coastline of South Africa, a group of people reported seeing an old vessel drifting eerily across the horizon, only to disappear without trace.

Of course, not every claimed sighting of the *Dutchman* can be taken at face value. The oceans, particularly at night, can play tricks on tired eyes and nervous dispositions. But in the end, there are just too many credible sightings – many by respectable men like Prince George, other Royal Navy officers and German U-Boat commanders – to simply reject the story of the *Flying Dutchman* out of hand. The mystery, like the ghost ship itself, will most likely go on forever.

While the *Flying Dutchman* is the most notorious of all shipbound ghost stories, it is by no means the only one. Consider the case of the large American vessel, the *St Paul*, which was involved in two tragic accidents, including a disastrous collision with the British cruiser, HMS *Gladiator*. Even today, the story of the *St Paul* continues to mystify, and dozens of 'earthly explanations' have been dismissed.

It was Thursday, 25 April 1918. The Great War was still waging across Europe, and America, which by now had thrown its full military muscle into the all-out conflict against the Kaiser's Germany, was busy refitting its cruise line ships into troop transport vessels. One such ship was the *St Paul*, a massive steamer which had once been the pride of the America Fleet. Early that morning, when the lengthy conversion work had been completed, the vessel set steam from its mooring at the Brooklyn docks for the short sail to Pier 61 on the Hudson River, on the west side of Manhattan. As the ship swung into the Hudson, Captain A.R. Mills noticed she was listing slightly to her port side.

The ghost ship has been blamed for several bizarre mishaps over the years, including shipwrecks.

AN UNEXPLAINED INCIDENT

He gave it little thought, however, assuming the crew were still filling the ballast tanks. When the ship approached the pier, two cables leading from the bow and the stern were thrown to the dock and secured. But as the *St Paul's* giant winches began to pull in the cables, the vessel began to list further. Suddenly and inexplicably, tons of water began to pour into her lower decks, forcing the boat onto her side, her towering masts scraping along the pier. Men began pouring over the sides, but fortunately, several tugs and a number of barges were close by, and rescued hundreds as they scrambled to safety. The incident could have been a major disaster if not for that stroke of good luck, and as a result, just four of the 400 men aboard were lost.

Initially, the investigation into the accident centred on German sabotage, but it was quickly ruled out. So, too, were dozens of other theories offered by everyone from old salts to the local newspapers. The real cause, however, was a shocker – when divers were sent into the river, they found that one of the ash ports close to the water line had not been closed! Every member of the crew was quizzed by the investigators, yet no-one was ever blamed for the error and to this day, the mystery of the open port has never been solved.

However, there was one other possibility – it might have been the sinister ghost of a dead sailor! To those who believe this to be the case, the timing of the disaster is the key. Because exactly ten years earlier – to the very day and to the very hour – the *St Paul* had been involved in a fatal collision with HMS *Gladiator*. Did a malevolent spirit choose that day, the tenth anniversary of the collision, to strike back? The accident involving the British cruiser occurred off the still waters of Southampton, when the *St Paul* was still a passenger liner.

The fog was so heavy that the two ships remained invisible to each other until they were less than half a mile apart. Once it was realized that a disaster was about to strike, Captain Walter Lumsden ordered evasive action, as did the pilot of the *St Paul*. Tragically, there was a miscalculation. Captain Lumsden ordered his ship hard-a-starboard, which left the *St Paul* heading directly towards her. A few minutes later, the inevitable occurred, as the mighty steamer ripped into the cruiser's starboard side. Twenty-seven of her crew were lost. At the inquiry that followed, Captain Lumsden was severely reprimanded by an Admiralty court martial, even though many considered his actions to have been the correct ones given the circumstances that day.

As we said earlier, ten years later to the hour of the disaster, an unseen hand opened the ash port aboard the *St Paul*, sending her to the bottom of the Hudson river. Mere coincidence?

A MYSTERY AT SEA

Derelict ships were not uncommon in the 19th century, but when the Mary Celeste *was found abandoned no one could understand what had happened to its crew . . . especially as their breakfast had not had time to go cold. The story of the* Mary Celeste *is considered by many to be one of the most intriguing and confusing mysteries in the annals of maritime history.*

The *Mary Celeste*, originally named the Amazon, set sail in 1872 for a trip across the Atlantic, but that was the last time her crew would ever be seen. The *Mary Celeste* was a proud brigantine, with two masts, weighing 282 tons and 103 feet long. She was built in Canada at Spencer's Island, Nova Scotia, the first ship of its kind to be built there. However, the *Mary Celeste* seemed to have a jinx, and crews were cautious of taking work on board the ship, despite the fact that she was in tip-top condition. Her first captain, R. Mclellan died on the ship's maiden voyage in 1867, after the *Mary Celeste* ran aground at Cape Breton.

A NEW CAPTAIN

One year later, the owners of the *Mary Celeste* appointed a new captain for their ship. They chose 37-year-old Benjamin Spooner Briggs, a man who was known for his sobriety and impeccable sense of judgement; a courageous man of whom it was said: 'would not abandon his vessel unless it was to save his own life'. The second-in-command, or mate, chosen for the voyage, was a man named Albert Richardson, who was also considered to be very qualified for the job.

The remaining crew of seven were chosen carefully for their experience,

Benjamin Spooner Briggs

due to the fact they were carrying a valuable cargo – 1,700 barrels of alcohol – which was valued at over $34,000. Their destination was Genoa, Italy and a return journey to New York with another valuable cargo had been prearranged. Briggs decided it would be a fine opportunity to take his wife, Sarah, and their two-year-old daughter, Sophie, with him on the trip as the weather forecast was good and he could not foresee any difficulties with the journey.

UNDER SAIL

The *Mary Celeste* set sail from New York on 7 November 1872, with its valuable cargo being shipped by Meissner Ackermann & Co. The cargo itself had been insured in Europe and the vessel by an American company. The ship rose and fell in the gentle swell of the Atlantic ocean and in the evening Sarah would play her harmonica while the rest of the crew accompanied her in song.

Following the path of the *Mary Celeste* was another ship called the *Dei Gratia*, which was carrying a cargo of 1,735 barrels of petroleum. They left New York on 15 November, but on the afternoon of 5 December, half way between the Azores and the Portuguese coast, their lookout spotted a brigantine floating mysteriously towards them. The captain on board the *Dei Gratia*, Captain Morehouse, recognised the ship as the *Mary Celeste*, but was surprised to see the ship yawing unsteadily into the wind, apparently out of control. Morehouse had dined with Briggs before they had embarked on their journey and was well aware of his fine reputation as a sailor.

They kept watch on the *Mary Celeste* for the next couple of hours, but after seeing no distress signals, nor getting any reply, the captain told his crew to man one of the small lifeboats.

The crew of the Dei Gratia *spotted the* Mary Celeste *floating mysteriously with no sign of a crew on board.*

Oliver Deveau, chief mate, and two other men, rowed towards the drifting ship and pulled up alongside. The *Mary Celeste* was creaking as she rode the waves and her sails were reduced to take advantage of the moderate breeze. The men's first thought was that the crew had contracted Yellow Jack, also known as American fever, but not a living soul could be seen on board.

The *Mary Celeste* was still in first class condition, with the hull, masts and sails all sound. The barrels of alcohol were still lashed in place in the hold and there were plentiful supplies of food and water. The sextant and chronometer were missing and the ship was awash with water. The captain's navigational equipment was nowhere to be found and it appeared some effort had been made to batten up the hatches.

When Deveau studied the captain's log, he found the last entry was written on 24 November, ten days earlier. This reported the ship's position as being just north of St Mary's

Island in the Azores, more than 400 miles from where it had been found.

This meant that the *Mary Celeste* had been drifting unmanned for a week and a half, and yet this could not have been possible because the ship was found with its sails set to catch the wind from the starboard side. The *Dei Gratia*, which had been following a parallel course, had their sails set for the port side, which meant it would have been impossible for the *Mary Celeste* to get to that position with its sails set to starboard. Someone must have still been on board the ship for at least several days after that final entry for the ship to have been found where it was.

Not one of the ten people that set sail on the *Mary Celeste* was ever found. Dozens of theories arose, ranging from attacking monsters from the deep, kidnap by aliens, piracy and even supernatural forces, but no one has ever found any evidence of what really happened. The yawl boat, a small four-oared boat carried over the main hatch, was missing, which suggested that at least some of the missing people could have got off the *Mary Celeste*.

The official report put out at the time by the British and American authorities, was that the crew had got at the alcohol, murdered the captain and his family, and then escaped in the yawl boat. However, there were no visible signs of any violence on board the ship and, if the crew had managed to escape, surely they would have turned up somewhere.

In 1913, an article was published in *Strand* magazine alleging that a man named Abel Fosdyke had been a secret passenger on that fateful voyage. However, his story was full of inconsistencies and didn't make sense. So, to this day, the mystery of the *Mary Celeste* remains unsolved. The only entity that can tell you the truth of what really happened is the *Mary Celeste* herself – and she won't talk!